If You Talk to Animals

If You Talk to Animals

◆

The Life of a Wildlife Rehabilitator

Cecilia Sanders

Ray

Thank you for loving the "wild" ones.

Cec Sanders

iUniverse, Inc.

New York Lincoln Shanghai

If You Talk to Animals
The Life of a Wildlife Rehabilitator

iUniverse, Inc.

For information address:
iUniverse, Inc.
2021 Pine Lake Road, Suite 100
Lincoln, NE 68512
www.iuniverse.com

The following is a true story. The names of the characters have not been changed to protect the innocent. They are the innocent.

ISBN: 0-595-33065-7

Printed in the United States of America

For Jessica

The following is a true story. The names of the characters have not been changed to protect the innocent. They are the innocent.

Contents

INTRODUCTION

My husband Tom and I are licensed wildlife rehabilitators with the Colorado Division of Wildlife. Our purpose is to take orphaned or injured wildlife, nurture it, and release the animal back into its natural way of life. We both have the innate desire to keep wild animals in their natural surroundings. To imprison a wild creature in a cage or to keep it as a pet is an inexcusable act.

Our work is strictly volunteer. We are not reimbursed for our expenses by the state of Colorado. Both of us are very fortunate to have excellent jobs that allow us to pursue and support our dreams. Our jobs also give us the needed time in the summer when we receive most of our animals. Tom is a high school science teacher and I teach elementary physical education.

During our twelve years as rehabilitators we have worked with and met many wonderful people. Many of them have given us monetary assistance or have helped out with necessities, such as dog food, fruit, and grain, to give our orphans a good start on life. We have had the pleasure of dealing with numerous veterinarians who have been most generous with their expertise and their services. The game wardens whom we have met have been most supportive. They show a genuine interest in wildlife. Many will drive hundreds of miles to relay an animal to us. Our mothers are probably our strongest supporters. Even though we have not given them human grandchildren, I believe that both of them have greatly enjoyed knowing many of their special "grandchildren".

I know that I will be criticized for being too anthropomorphic in my writing of animals. That is ascribing human characteristics to nonhuman things. Any one who spends time with animals and cannot see the uniqueness in each individual, does not deserve to be around them. To some people anthropomorphism is an undesirable quality. To me it is a gift. Animals have personalities just as people do. In many instances they have much more pleasant attributes than some people.

What harm is there in placing human characteristics on animals? None, as long as placing these characteristics on them is not carried to the point where the animals suffer. If anthropomorphism becomes illegal, I will be the first to be arrested.

One of the questions that we are most frequently asked is, "You must get so attached to your animals, how can you let them go"? We live with them and are very much attached to them. We do not own them, we simply experience them and we learn from them. The ultimate reward in what we do is to let them be free.

FOREWORD

If you love something, set it free.
If it comes back to you, it is yours.
If it doesn't, it never was.

The creatures that we have shared our lives with over the last several years have inspired me to write the following story. They have given us the strength to deal with almost any situation that arises. Their life and death existence has changed our perception of life. There have been many times that we have cried so hard that we swore that we would never take another animal. There have been times that we have laughed so hard that we cried.

Looking back over the years, I know that the laughter and the joys greatly outweigh the sorrow and the pain. I try to be realistic about what we attempt to accomplish and I know that what we give our animals and share with them is a very special gift. I know that I cannot protect them forever, I do not want to.

Even though their lives are often short, we give them a quality life. They are given everything that they need, the greatest being the chance to be themselves, to live in their world, take their chances and to be free. We do love them all. We do set them free. Some of them come back to us and depend on us longer than others and in a sense they really are ours, but only temporarily. A neighbor once asked me, "Are all of the deer in the area yours?" My reply was, "No, they are not mine, they are only friends."

Every summer when we begin to feel that we cannot keep up the hectic pace, we try to convince ourselves that perhaps we should take a year off. After things slow down during the winter months I find myself counting the days until we begin receiving our first orphans. I can't even imagine spending my life without these magnificent creatures. Life would be very dull. Perhaps a day will come when we cannot do what we have dedicated our lives to. We have found it impossible to say no.

My story includes only a handful of the creatures that have enhanced our lives over the last several years. What you are about to read is about the last five years of our work as wildlife rehabilitators. The story begins with the first fawns that we were able to release and watch evolve into wild animals in the area in which we live.

"If you talk to animals they will talk to you and you will know each other. If you do not talk to them you will not know them and what you do not know you will fear. What one fears one destroys."
Chief Dan George

1

TIM AND TIM

With only two days left until summer vacation, we kept our fingers crossed in hopes that no fawns would arrive until school was dismissed. Our luck did not last. On June second, 1987, about 5:00 P.M. the game warden phoned and said that he would be bringing us a newborn fawn. At seven o'clock he arrived with the baby mule deer resting in a cardboard box in the back of his pickup truck. The little buck had experienced a long journey that day, about two hundred miles. He needed to be fed. The first of the spring fawns are always so tiny and helpless, yet so trusting. It is as if they are saying, "Well, I'm here. Feed me!" He drained his eight-ounce bottle of specially formulated doe milk and bedded down for the night in our intensive care room.

The next day turned out to be cold and rainy and we wanted very badly to stay home with him, but he would have to travel again. He would have to go back to school with us since he had to be fed every four hours. The little buck traveled quietly and spent a peaceful day in the confines of my small office. One more day!

Late that afternoon the game warden called and reported that two more fawns were awaiting us at the wildlife office. We would pick them up on our way home. Excited about our little buck having company, we eagerly entered the office to meet the twins. To add to our joy, they were antelope twins.

That evening we were back home with one working day left, one little mule deer and two very stubborn, uncooperative antelope babies. They did not trust us at all and would not take a bottle from someone who was so strange. During the night the two were tube fed every four hours and then were packed up for their last day of traveling.

Tom had the pleasure of taking them with him for the last day. We arrived early, entered the school building and headed for the elevator. He was carrying a box of

1

antelope and I had a box containing a deer. No one knew the contents of the boxes as we traveled up five stories to his office.

Being as young as they were, the fawns were quite content with eating and staying quiet, just as they would in nature when their mothers hide them, leave, and return only to feed them. They are scentless so they do not attract predators.

Tom was successful with getting the twins to take a few ounces from the bottle and they were much stronger than they had been the night before. Little did we know at the time that they would never trust us or accept us as surrogate antelope. Another trip and they could settle in to spend the summer with us and then return to their prairie home.

The little buck became known as Tim for reasons that I will explain later. The antelope twins were named Dan and Diane, DanTelope and DianTelope. The twins finally recognized us as their only food source but were not going to be very cooperative about the matter. Every feeding was a contest to see what horrible contortions they could get our bodies into before accepting the bottle. They seemed to totally enjoy seeing me in severe pain, stretching, bending and holding the bottle out to them until hunger finally won over.

Tim, our little buck, was the exact opposite. He aimed to please. He was getting more active now and spent more time showing us how he could stand on top of the bales of hay and the cardboard boxes that concealed Dan and Diane.

The time came to move the trio outdoors. We have a very large chain link pen where the fawns can get used to the outdoors yet still be safe from predators. From the pen they graduate to the yard, which gives them access to their natural lives.

I was not looking forward to the move outdoors. Tim simply followed us out eagerly and cooperatively. Dan and Diane, however, at eight pounds each ranked right up there with professional rodeo stock.

The two were enclosed in their boxes and carried out to the pen. I waited for the explosion but when the boxes were opened they simply stepped out, looked around, and seemed perfectly satisfied. Now they could stay farther away from us.

June twenty-first brought us yet another set of twins, tiny mule deer twins who tipped the scale at three pounds each. The two were very eager to eat and were left to settle down in the intensive care room. The twins became known as Tiny Tim and Little Doe Peep. We now had Tim Buck One and Tim Buck Two.

Because of their size the little twins spent the night in the intensive care room. In the outdoor pen that they visited during the day they could easily walk through the opening between the fence and the gate.

As the summer passed Big Tim (Tim Buck One) spent most of the day out of the pen. He would hide in the scrub oak until I called him to come out and have his bottle. After nursing he would return to the safety of his hiding place. At night he would join the others in the closed pen.

Dan and Diane

Dan and Diane would now come to be fed but only after they carefully scrutinized me. Diane could now successfully flatten three eight-ounce bottles of milk. She would then smile her crooked little smile, totally pleased that I was partially paralyzed from the position that she had managed to get me to assume. This happened four times daily.

As the summer passed, feeding times became less frequent and at last everyone was weaned. Tim Buck One, Tim Buck Two and Little Doe Peep spent more time out of the pen, chasing each other and playing deer games.

About the middle of August Diane managed to sneak out of the gate early one morning when I let the mule deer out. At first she just grazed and worked around the yard with the deer. Could I trust her? When the deer began running, Diane joined in and I began to relax. They disappeared behind the scrub oak across the road. Diane, being unfamiliar with the area, ran full speed into the wire fence nearby. Terrified and obviously injured she would not let me approach her. She bedded down in the thick brush and I left her alone hoping that at feeding time she would at least let us get close enough to catch her.

It was a long day. She was hungry but not enough to trust us. Finally, at nightfall, we managed to corner her and carry her to the pen. I felt sick. Why did I let her out? I slept with her in the shelter in the pen until about midnight when it began to rain.

The injury was much more serious than I had thought. Her spine was severely injured and she was no longer able to stand or lift her head. We carried her to the indoor room and made her as comfortable as we could, propping her neck and head up with blankets and straw. This was not the Diane that I knew, the Diane that could make a pretzel out of me. She just lay there and let me touch her.

Our vet suggested an injection to reduce any inflammation on her spine that could be causing her paralysis. Diane died in my arms that second night. Tears streamed down my face as I cradled the beautiful antelope doe who kept her dignity to her last breath. I felt like such a failure. Dan was now alone! How would he react?

The next morning when I went out to the pen to feed there was a pit in the bottom of my stomach. How could I explain to Dan? He came for his bottles and curiously looked around. I tried to explain to him what had happened. He knew. How could I be foolish enough to think that I could talk to something as superior as he was?

Tim, Tim, and Little Doe Peep were roaming freely. I kept Dan in the pen until the middle of November when he was relocated in antelope country. When we opened the carrier, Dan came out, flared his white rump patch, crawled through a fence, and left without looking back. The two should have gone together but there was nothing that I could do now. He, I'm sure was glad to be rid of us. The two Tims and Little Doe Peep were to stay and share with us their beautiful transition into the real world of deer.

2

GROWING UP

Living in the foothills, we have many deer that frequent our yard to forage. Our fawns were accustomed to visits by them since their first days with us. Although they had been taken away from their real mothers, they could still see their relatives. As they spent more time on their own they began to move with the wild deer.

In the beauty of their first fall I can remember many walks through the colorful oak brush with the three of them tagging along. When we would come across a group of wild deer we would sit back and let the trio approach them and interact. It was a very special event to witness.

One day in late October I awoke to find Doe Peep feverish and very weak. I called off work and took her indoors to make her more comfortable. Shortly after seven o'clock she died. We suspected her death was caused by pneumonia. Little Doe Peep was a beautiful loving little creature who had enhanced our lives for the last four months. She left memories that we will never forget.

After the hunting season Tim and Tim were not shut in at night and spent most of their time with the wild herd. Each evening, however, they returned for a snack of apples and grain. As the days grew shorter and colder, the only evidence of them was their small hoof prints going into the barn to get treats and then going back out.

Tim & Tim

On Thanksgiving night as we cross country skied in the full moonlight, the two Tims trailed along romping and chasing each other in the snow. I can still feel the joy that we experienced that night. Christmas Eve found them peering through the large windows at the brightly-lit tree.

During the months of January and February they moved with the herd to winter pasture and other creatures dominated our lives. Everyday I looked for the tiny hoof prints, but they weren't there. Thinking of them often and praying for their safety, we felt very satisfied that we had accomplished what we had set out to do; let them return to their natural way of life.

On the first day of spring vacation, during the last week of March, I was out in the open front barn doing my chores when I heard a noise behind me. I turned and to my surprise it was Tiny Tim, shaggy and thin, with his big wide eyes try-ing to tell me something. In a startled voice I said, "Timmy, where is Big Tim?" I stepped around the corner of the barn to see Tim nibbling at the young tender spring grasses. He looked up as I spoke to him and then limped over to see me. On his back right leg was a deep five-inch long cut.

He let me inspect, clean, and dress the wound. He also had three long scrapes along his right side. We strongly suspected that he had been in the grips of a mountain lion who had reached for him as he fled.

From that day he and Tiny Tim spent about a month at home, even returning to the safety of their pen that was left open. He kept the wound clean by licking it and it healed very nicely. He really seemed to appreciate all the attention that he was getting. Tiny Tim remained a faithful friend but was getting impatient and soon the two rejoined their herd and we saw them less frequently.

With the onset of spring we could expect almost anything since we have gained the reputation of being sincere rehabilitators. April and May brought us the usual foxes and raccoons. Our yearling bucks were doing well and we saw them less and less. We wondered what the coming summer would bring.

3

THE ODD COUPLE

School was dismissed for summer vacation on June second and we were enjoying the freedom that we knew could not last. June ninth brought us our first fawn, a petite, fragile Whitetail doe who became known as Jessica Fawn. The moment she was placed on the floorboard of my Bronco she drank her bottle and off we drove to her new home.

Jessica was housed in the intensive care room and fed every four hours. She then returned to her well-manicured nest of straw to wait for her mother to return. Being strong and healthy she was taken out to the yard for short excursions after each feeding, readily returning to her nest afterwards. We were still very relaxed and everything was going very smoothly.

June twelfth brought Jessica her friend and companion for the next six months. At 6:00 p.m. we received a call. A two-day-old bull elk calf had been found entangled in a barbed wire fence and was in very bad shape. Would we consider taking on the responsibility of trying to raise him?

It took less than a fraction of a second for our response. We were to meet the game warden at ten o'clock that night. She would have to drive several hours to pick him up and bring him to us.

The time went by slowly as we prepared for his arrival. We gathered the items necessary for his survival. Knowing that he was weak, we tried to prepare ourselves for the fact that he might not even make it to us.

We arrived at our meeting place about thirty minutes early, well armed with a large bottle of warm fluids and the equipment to tube feed him. When dehydrated as severely as we knew he was, fluids were an absolute necessity for his survival.

Parked on the side of the highway, we laughed at the thought of a State Patrol-man checking to see why we had stopped there. I am thankful that we did not have to explain the situation to anyone.

The game warden finally arrived with "Larry," our little Lawrence Elk. He was a huge two-day-old spotted baby weighing at least forty pounds. He was very dehy-drated, had numerous cuts, and was unable to nurse or stand. Within minutes he was in the back of my Bronco. We had long ago stripped it of a useless back seat and replaced it with a large thick foam pad for occasions such as this.

His only chance now was to be kept warm, hydrated, and comfortable. We drove off eager to get him home when the question occurred, "What in the world do you do with a forty pound bull elk calf?" We would do our best.

The drive home took about twenty minutes. Because of his weakened state, we decided not to move him again until morning, if he managed to hang on that long. I curled up next to him on the thick foam pad to keep him warm. His breathing was very labored, and I was not very optimistic. We slept as good as could be expected.

Once during the night he awakened me by standing, turning around, and lying down again. Things were looking better. He was obviously much stronger than he had been a few hours ago and we both fell fast asleep. About four o'clock Larry decided that he no longer wanted to be held hostage in the back of my truck. Pushing on the windows with his lacerated nose he wanted nothing to do with me. He wanted OUT.

I wrestled with him for awhile but he had no intention of lying down again. I didn't want to leave him in the truck alone to go for help. After being tangled in a fence, I'm sure being trapped by a steering wheel wouldn't have made him any happier.

I began calling for Tom, who I knew would be coming soon to check on us. It didn't take long for him to come to my rescue. We wrapped Larry in a heavy blanket and carried him to the shelter in the chain link pen. The little wooden shelter soon became known as the local "Elks lodge".

Being outdoors seemed to calm him down and he settled in nicely in the deep straw bedding. Knowing that he was much stronger, I was able to get another hour of rest. When I went out to check on him he had come out of the shelter and was lying down in the tall grass. He was easy to approach but not interested in the bottle that was offered to him. His increased strength made it difficult to tube feed him and before each feeding an attempt was made to get him to nurse a bottle. We tried everything, pop bottles with lamb nipples, baby bottles with lamb nipples, baby bottles with baby nipples. All he would do was lay there and hold the nipple in his mouth with milk running down his neck and my arms, as I became more frustrated.

Even minor signs of impatience were beginning to show in my even-tempered husband. Larry wasn't fighting us, he just wasn't swallowing. We even purchased a huge bottle and nipple for feeding baby calves. No Luck. It just looked even more ridiculous sticking out of his mouth and was much more difficult to hold.

Finally on day three I poured the milk into a large stainless steel pan and offered it to him. He immersed his entire face into the milk and drained every drop. Then he lifted his head and let me wipe all the excess milk from his face. He looked up and seemed to smile with his huge bottom teeth protruding as if he were saying, "Ah, that was delicious!" The battle was over. Feeding time now was fun, not exasperating. He was consuming one and a half gallons of milk a day, smiling contentedly after each feeding.

After each meal it was necessary to stimulate his rectal area with a warm paper towel so that he would have a bowel movement. His mother would do this by licking him. I wasn't quite up to doing that. This was necessary until he was eliminating on his own. We could have easily purchased a paper towel factory, or at least bought stock in one.

Larry spent most of his time in the elk lodge with short journeys into the pen to stretch a bit and eat some fresh dirt. We have found that most fawns seem to enjoy doing this. After strolling around he would return to the safety of the large nest in the shelter.

It was now time to introduce Jessica to Larry. He was out for his after dinner stroll and Jessica had finished her bottle, so I let her come down to the pen for a formal introduction.

Jessica at the time had a large amount of confidence in herself and immediately walked up to him and tried to nurse. After all, he was large enough to be her mother. She topped out at his knee. Larry was frightened of her and quickly returned to his shelter leaving her to explore the pen.

As the days progressed Jessica was allowed to spend more time in the pen with Larry. At night she returned to her indoor shelter. Larry was beginning to figure out the feeding routine from watching Jessica. After each bottle Jessica would suck on my ear lobes until she was satisfied. All of our fawns have done this and I laughed at the thought of Larry doing it.

One day when Jessica came out to the pen everything seemed to click inside Larry's head and his usual passive mood exploded. He ran across the pen, threw himself on his knees, dove under Jessica and tried to nurse her. He lifted her off the ground, determined to eat, and suddenly realized that I was there with his pan of milk. He dove into the milk, drained the bucket and then attached himself to my ear. He nursed and nursed as the leftover milk ran down my neck and into my hair. I was being paid the ultimate compliment. I was now a "cow elk" and would be for the next six months.

Larry was a gentleman as he nursed my ear lobe, but a very sloppy gentleman. The paper towel consumption doubled because I also had to be cleaned up after each feeding. I never really minded. For some reason he needed that few moments of contact and I was not going to take it away from him. It had now turned into a ritual and I must confess that I probably enjoyed it as much as he did.

4

THE RETURN OF THE TIMS

One morning about the middle of June, I was in the pen just enjoying the quiet day. Larry was in his lodge and Jess was concealed in the tall grasses. I heard a noise in the scrub oak outside the pen and turned to see Big Tim nonchalantly stroll out of the brush and go to the back of the pen that he had occupied only a year ago. He had come to meet the new occupants.

I hadn't seen him for almost six weeks. He had lost his shaggy winter coat and replaced it with his new summer attire. His antlers had grown to about eight inches long and were covered with lush velvet. He was absolutely magnificent. I watched motionless to see what was going to happen.

Jessica immediately picked up on the visitor and tiptoed over to meet this hand-some gent. They sniffed noses through the fence and he seemed to be telling her that she was in good hands and that when she was out he would show her his world. The visits became routine. Tim would arrive after sun up, come out of the scrub oak after each feeding and then leave at night.

I was becoming a bit concerned that I had not seen Little Tim (Tim Buck Two) for quite some time. During my visits with Big Tim I would talk to him and tell him to please bring Little Tim home for his birthday, which was June twenty-first. I just wanted to see him and be assured of his safety.

On the morning of the twenty-first, I was sitting on the deck before sunrise and saw two young deer approaching the yard. One seemed to be coaxing the other one along. As they got closer to the house, I could tell that they were bucks and quickly recognized the smaller of the two as Tiny Tim. Big Tim was about twenty-five feet behind him and seemed to be saying to him, "Come on Timmy. It's your birthday, and she did ask me to bring you home. Please go."

Little Tim reluctantly approached. His large brown eyes expressed the fact that he really did not want to be there but Big Tim made him come and he was not going to stay very long. With a tear stained face I greeted him, thanked him for coming, and wished him a beautiful day. The little buck seemed somewhat embarrassed and eagerly left. I also thanked Big Tim who seemed ever so proud of himself. Moments such as these are treasures in my mind.

Little Tim was now visiting the yard more frequently but was not very excited about the new tenants. In fact, he seemed a bit jealous. When Big Tim came to the back of the pen, Jessica would quickly get up and seemed to say "Look Larry! Big Tim is here." The two would then visit with him through the fence.

Now that Jessica was spending more time out of the pen she could visit Tim without the fence between them. I was concerned at first, but he didn't bother her at all.

I was quite apprehensive about letting Larry out. I was afraid that he might think that our horses were his family and take up residence with them. The time was going to have to come. He was growing very rapidly and was going to need more room.

The main reason that Jessica spent so much time out of the pen was because I lived in fear of Larry squashing her. Playtime was terrifying, but Jess always seemed to out maneuver him until he was just too tired to play.

We decided to see what would happen if we let him out to explore the yard with her. He was so attached to her that he quickly fell into her routine of hiding in the scrub oak until it was time to be fed. All that I had to do was announce that I was available with two baby bottles and a large, red, heart-shaped bucket that Larry had graduated to.

As soon as they heard my voice, we would all race to the pen to dine. His table manners were atrocious to say the least. He drank with his entire face submerged. I had to brace the bucket because he would punch it first, spraying milk everywhere and then inhale the rest. He could drink a gallon before Jess finished her sixteen ounces.

I was armed with several paper towels ready to grasp his face and absorb leftovers before he could firmly attach himself to my ear. Jess would already be frantically sucking the other one. After faces were scrubbed and instincts satisfied, both of them would slip away into their nests or on hot days they would disappear into the coolness of the thickets of tall grasses and shrubs.

In the corner of their pen we kept a big bed of fresh straw in which they spent much of their time. Lying side by side, they would groom each other and nap. Each had their own spot and when the nests were not occupied it was obvious which one belonged to whom. By August the two were being fed twice daily, once in the early morning and again at dusk.

Feeding time was my favorite time of day. It made me feel good to give them something that they appreciated and looked forward to so much. The later it got in the day the closer the two would get to the feeding station. As they rested patiently I would sneak into the house and prepare their milk, which was freshly mixed each time. When I felt that it was time, I would quietly go out the front door and get as close as I could to the pen before they heard me. Once they heard or saw me the race was on.

I seriously considered buying a pair of large rubber ears from a novelty shop to save my ears. This idea was abandoned when I had visions of the game warden driving up as I was racing a deer and an elk, carrying pink and blue baby bottles, a large, red, heart-shaped bucket, paper towels flowing from my back pockets and wearing huge rubber ears. I certainly wouldn't want to give someone the impression that I wasn't playing with a full deck.

The odd couple were getting much braver and wandering farther from home. Larry was extremely fond of Jessica and would not let her out of his sight. Wherever Jess went, Larry did too. The two were quite a sight. Larry easily weighed one hundred and fifty pounds by now and Jessica about twenty. I get very involved with them and as they roamed farther and farther, I worried more and more.

Jessica knew exactly what she could do to make me a nervous wreck. One of her favorite tricks was to lead her big friend over to stand in the middle of the road. It is just a small dirt road and very few cars use it, but they needed to be afraid of vehicles and I tried my darndest to frighten them.

One morning they bedded down facing the road about seventy-five yards away. I got into my bronco and drove up and down the road, honking, gunning the motor, and slamming on the brakes and sliding. I would drive down the road about one hundred yards and then backup making assorted noises. The two just calmly watched me make a fool of myself, chewing their cuds and looking as though they were watching a tennis match.

Things have a way of working themselves out. They didn't need me. They had this road thing all figured out and could tell if a car was coming a mile away and would bound to safety if they felt threatened.

To give an idea of their size difference, late one afternoon the telephone company repairman came to service our phone. Larry and Jessica were out grazing in the front yard. I was with them but not visible to the repairman. I watched as he slowly drove into the yard staring at the two, parked his truck and went into the house, never taking his eyes off them.

Several minutes later he returned to his truck and drove away, staring even harder and looking very confused. Later while talking to Tom, I understood the confused look on the poor man's face. The repairman had told him that there was a doe and a fawn in our front yard. Tom simply replied that, "No, it wasn't a doe and fawn; it was a fawn and an elk calf." He didn't explain why they were there.

As the summer was quickly coming to an end, Larry and Jessica were heading off into the mountains every day, but bounding home for their evening milk. They were no longer being shut in at night and I shivered to think of where Jessica was taking Larry while I lay fast asleep. At least I couldn't worry while I slept and I was sure that Jessica could handle even the toughest of situations.

They were always home in the morning. Hoping to wean them soon, I began watering down their milk, but they still drank as feverishly now as ever. After eating they would return to the places that were becoming more important to them.

Larry & Jessica

Larry was not very adept at going through fences. Maybe it was his original predicament that kept him from being sure about them. One day after he managed to get through the fence across the road, he was having a difficult time coming back through. I went over and tried to help him solve his problem. As I was down on my hands and knees crawling back and forth through the bottom two wires, I was totally unaware that my neighbor was watching in amazement. Larry finally got the idea, crawled under the wire after me, and then followed me home. My neighbor just drove by shaking his head.

One morning as Tom and I were going to work, Larry and Jessica were crossing through the llama pasture and the fence again confused him. We drove back into the yard, got a pair of wire cutters and returned to cut the center wire, making a nice big opening for him. He never forgot that opening and to this day I think every deer in the vicinity uses it for easy access to our yard.

At three months Larry was easily the size of the large does and larger than most of the yearling bucks. As he would approach the herd, they couldn't quite figure out what he was.

He and Jess would follow us on our walks up the mountain. We would find a nice spot to sit and watch the two introduce themselves. By late summer the herd accepted them. They were now living two separate lives, one with the wild deer and one with us. When we walked or watched for them through binoculars, we would see them starting their real lives just as Tim and Tim had done the year before. I knew that they should be weaned soon but I also wanted to keep them close to home until after the hunting season.

I suppose that it seems a bit strange that a Whitetail doe and a bull elk calf were living with a herd of mule deer. It would only be a temporary way of life. We felt that it was very important for them to have a closer relationship with animals than with people and this was obviously beginning to happen. In time they would meet their own kind. It would also make it a lot easier for me to monitor them.

My neighbor, who is very supportive of what we do, told me one day, "It is such a treat to drive by and see a herd of deer with Larry right there among them, kind of like a redwood tree."

Jess was easy to spot because she was the only Whitetail for miles around. Her large erect white tail gave her away instantly when the herd was frightened and felt the need to flee.

When the two did spend time around the house Larry would walk on the large wood deck that we have with firewood storage underneath. He thought it was great fun to pull the logs out and drop them. Tennis shoes were another one of his favorite things. He would pick them up by the strings and spin them or beat them against the side of the house.

Windows were a real fascination. Some mornings I would come downstairs and see his gigantic face staring in at me with his nose pressed against the glass. It was useless to wash windows. There would be time for that when he was gone.

Tom couldn't read a book or magazine without Larry trying to turn the pages. There were times when Larry wanted to play and the only sensible thing to do when this happened was to go into the house until the mood passed. He also liked to sip the sweet nectar from the humming "elk" feeder.

Larry was easily pushing three hundred pounds by late November and was not what I really considered a playmate. Jessica could handle these moods better than I. Her size and quick moves enabled her to dodge him and when things got tense, duck into the scrub oak and lose him. During playtime, we went indoors to watch through the windows and then safely returned outdoors when they were finished.

I knew that it was time to wean them. They were drinking water with only the slightest hint of milk. I had finally run out of my powdered milk and tried to fool them with canned goat milk. It didn't bother Jessica a bit. Larry, however, was not going to be fooled.

I marched outside one evening with his bucket and placed it in the gravel driveway. He came skidding in as usual, starved to death, threw himself on his knees, buried his face in the bucket and withdrew with a horrified look. He was positive that I was trying to poison him. He just lay there with his heart broken and pouted. Good! I thought. He's weaned. Not so! For the next two weeks he drank water, pure, plain, warm water twice a day.

This was ridiculous. I was never going to get him weaned. I was beginning to be afraid of him. Even after a tasteless dinner of warm water we still went through the ear sucking ritual. The only problem now was that it was the middle of November and a bit cold out for having water dribble down your face and neck.

I was beginning to get frightened when I read that some cow elk allow their offspring to nurse until they are nine months old. I vividly imagined that and decided that something had to be done. Larry must have been getting tired of the whole thing also.

It happened early one morning as I faithfully went out the door with the infamous red, heart-shaped bucket. It had snowed the night before and Larry and Jessica were in their playful mood. They wanted me to play, but seeing the look in Larry's eyes I knew that the only chance I had was to get back inside.

I quickly placed the bucket in the driveway and ran inside. A few minutes later when I returned, the only thing I saw was a puddle of water, no Larry, no Jessica, no red, heart-shaped bucket. I looked around and about thirty yards from the puddle were the red plastic remains. Larry had enough of the tasteless stuff and had put and end to it, bucket and all. He was finally weaned and I felt a lot safer.

After he was weaned, he became less dependent on us and spent more time away from home. The pattern was starting to form as it had with Tim and Tim one year ago. The only time Larry came to the yard was during the night and then it was only to feed on the succulent alfalfa hay in the barn. Every time I thought that they were getting wilder they would surprise me by coming and spending the entire day in the yard, basking the mild winter days away in the bushes.

On Thanksgiving Day the two stayed all day long and paid our mothers a visit late in the afternoon, Larry the gentleman, Jessica the busy body. Our mothers are very proud of the work that we do with the wild orphans and are pleased to have such unique "Grandchildren".

After Thanksgiving about the only time that we saw them was through telescopes or binoculars. If we were out walking or skiing, we would see them but they would not approach us. It was as though they were embarrassed that we were their parents, typical adolescents! We were very pleased to see this instinct in them.

Winter was approaching rapidly. The only sign of Larry was his giant hoof prints in the snow leading into the barn and then back out. Jessica was still making short visits twice a day. She had more important things to do.

Our feelings of success were at an all time high and we were looking forward to a relaxing two-week Christmas vacation. Unfortunately, it was not going to be the Christmas that we had planned.

5

LARRY SAYS GOOD BYE

Early on the morning of our first day of vacation we were leaving the yard on cross-country skis. As we skied past the llama corral, I noticed Briggs, our youngest llama standing in a very awkward position. I removed my skis and walked toward him. He was staggering and as I reached up to put a halter on him he screamed in pain and fell to the ground, never to stand again.

As I lay with him in the snow, cradling his head and neck, Tom ran inside to call our vet. With the help of our neighbor we slid the llama onto a sturdy piece of plywood and pulled him into the trailer. I didn't return to the house, still wearing my cross-country ski boots and jeans that were soaking wet from lying in the snow with him, I crawled into the trailer and supported his head and neck. Briggs was examined by our vet and arrangements were made to take him to a veterinary hospital over two hundred miles away.

It took us over five hours to reach the hospital. A two-hour detour through downtown Denver, Colorado was almost more than I could handle. I had no idea what was happening. All I could feel was the truck stopping and then slowly inching forward, stopping, and going forward again. Because Briggs had me trapped, I could not stand up to see what was happening. Finally, the truck and trailer gained speed steadily and I knew that we were on our way again. The long hours that I passed in the trailer were spent reminiscing about the special times that I had shared with him. Briggs was my first llama.

We arrived at the hospital just as the sun was setting. From where I lay in the trailer I could see and hear flocks of Canada geese flying south and secretly wished that I could escape with them.

After a lengthy examination and numerous x-rays, the vets could not explain the cause of the paralysis that Briggs was experiencing. They assured us that we would accomplish nothing by staying, and we were encouraged to return home.

We arrived home about two o'clock Sunday morning. One of our family was not with us and the outlook was very discouraging. The next four days were a nightmare and thoughts of Larry and Jessica were in the back of our minds. The usual excitement of Christmas was gone. I did things only because I had to, knowing deep down that our Briggs would never come home.

Daily reports from the hospital were not optimistic and on the fourth day, just three days before Christmas, our Briggs had to be euthanized. An autopsy could not pinpoint the exact cause of the paralysis.

Our remaining llama, Stratton, was upset and confused about what had been going on. We made arrangements with a friend to bring home a companion for him. The next day we made the two hundred-mile trip again, in silence, leaving long before sunrise. We had to return to the hospital to take care of things there, pick up our horse trailer, drive another forty miles to pick up the new llama and then return home. The day was very long and difficult and Larry and Jessica were not even on our minds.

We arrived home well after dark to a snow-covered yard and a brilliant full moon, sixty to seventy mile an hour winds accompanied us the last half our journey. Stratton was excited and got up to greet us as we pulled into the yard with the trailer. But a stranger, not his best friend, exited. We didn't want to introduce the two at this time. We would wait until morning when everyone was rested.

We decided to put "Parika" in the deer pen for the night. As I walked across the front yard leading him to his pen I noticed large hoof prints going into the pen. There in the light of the full moon stood a very large animal. Larry was in the deer pen. I hadn't seen him in over two weeks. I quickly turned and led Parika to another enclosure.

Larry followed and offered his sympathy in a most sincere way. He let me rub his head and neck as he reached up to give me a tiny ear nibble as if saying, "I knew you needed me". Suddenly the horrible day seemed to come to a miraculous ending. He was still here, Stratton and Jess were still here, and surely Briggs's memory would be here forever. Larry let me know this in his gentle way.

During the night I checked on Parika several times and noticed that Larry and Jessica were bedded down near his pen. In the morning the two returned to their other world. It was now time to pick up the pieces and try to get through Christmas. Just knowing that Stratton had company made it much easier to cope with. The two were getting along just fine.

For the last month or so I had been carrying hay to a pole barn about two hundred yards through our pasture. Larry, Jess, and their herd of mule deer friends dined there daily.

Early Christmas eve, I made my delivery. Jessica popped out of the brush and in a few minutes Larry appeared and was very cordial. I quickly came home to get Tom so that he could take a picture of him. By the time we returned, Larry had disappeared.

After dark on Christmas Eve we made a special delivery. We took hay, grain, apples and fresh water for the herd. Before sunrise on Christmas morning, we walked across our pasture toward the barn. Santa had visited the pole barn. The entire herd, including Tim and Tim were there enjoying the palatable gift they had received. We stopped so that we would not interfere. They too, froze and returned our stare. One by one they tiptoed off. Larry flared his rump patch and disappeared on the deer trail through the scrub oak. The only one left was petite little Jessica in her fine winter coat and a very puzzled look. "Where is every-body going?" she seemed to be saying. She stayed only a few moments and then followed the group.

A special Christmas after all! Four of the animals in the group were our hand raised orphans. It was truly a wonderful Christmas present to us, a priceless gift that cannot ever be taken away.

Christmas Day was the last time that we saw Larry. After Christmas he was seen with eleven mule deer. They had moved down the mountain and were feeding in the alfalfa fields. The sightings were less frequent now with the short, cold days of winter. We have never heard of anyone else seeing him again and are very hopeful that he had found and taken refuge with his own species. We thought of him often.

The following summer we followed a set of yearling elk tracks through the pasture that he used when we still knew him. Each big round hoof print brought back a memory of our Larry and all the silly things that he used to do. Maybe they weren't his, but we found great satisfaction in thinking and hoping that they were. He had chosen the life that he was born to live, the life of an elk, a real honest to goodness elk.

I think back on the question that entered our minds the night that we tube fed the weak creature in the back of my Bronco. What do you do with a bull elk calf? We did our best and we succeeded.

Jessica was very upset when he left but stayed on the mountain with the mule deer. She still fed nightly with them in the yard. We saw a lot of her through the winter. She was always ready to give me kisses and Tom a good shove or two.

6

THE NEW YEAR

January and February are usually very quiet months. We had been wintering a black bear cub since September. All that was necessary to keep him happy was lots of food and a good shelter. He would be released in the spring. April came and Boris the black bear was taken to a remote area and set free. His fat little body rippled as he ran for his freedom. Once again he could explore and climb.

March brought us our three new llamas. Zoom, a little male, and Tyche and Lada, two little females. We had plenty of time to spend walking with them and working with them. They are such beautiful, curious creatures.

Zoom, Tyche, & Lada

The llamas quickly became acquainted with Jessica, who had wintered well and was relishing the new tender grasses of early spring. She seemed so alone without her big friend, but kept the company of the mule deer.

Two days after we released our bear cub we received a call from a veterinary hospital in Cheyenne Wyoming, over two hundred miles away. The clinic rehabilitated birds of prey and didn't know what to do with a three-week-old red fox that someone had brought to them.

Gracie arrived the evening of April twelfth, a tiny handful of brown fuzz. She was not very happy about the all day car trip but settled down nicely in the intensive care room. The little fox immediately retreated to the den in the corner and settled on the heating pad that lined it.

Gracie was already eating by herself which made it easy to leave her during the day while we were still in school. At one month she was already very fond of mice and birds.

Frequently we have birds that fly into our large windows. These are frozen and used for training animals such as little foxes.

Her first human mother who had bottle-fed her had given her the name Gracie when she was one day old. Graceful, she was not. In fact she was a total klutz. Even as she grew up and was developing the skills of a fox, she would occasionally trip or stumble or jump too far and fall off the deck into the thick grass below.

As she grew up she was given the freedom of the greenhouse where she learned to become a very successful mouse hunter. She had dens under various things and could leap to the top of the cages that were kept in her domain.

When given the opportunity to visit the great outdoors, Gracie would sneak out the door a short distance and sniff the air. If frightened by some strange smell, she would race back to the safety of her den. Gracie gradually worked out farther and farther into the yard but returned indoors when not chaperoned by Tom or myself.

Gracie was afraid of the large tomcat that found his way to live in our barn. The cat would chase her back into the greenhouse during her outdoor excursions. One day I was outside with her but was busy doing something and not paying complete attention to her. Suddenly I heard a terrible commotion. The big tom-

cat had attacked Gracie and she raced back to the safety of her den. She was terri-
fied and would not come out.

Gracie

I wanted to know if she was injured and tried everything to get her to come out. I
tried coaxing her out with her favorite toys, food, even a fresh "birdcicle" (frozen
bird). Finally I lay down on my stomach and reached in to pull her out. She had
me totally convinced that she was not going to make it through such a terrible
ordeal. The happy little carefree fox had met someone who did not like her.

As I held her she pathetically held up her right front leg and whimpered. Her leg
was bruised and very sore, but the skin was not broken. Gracie was convinced
that she was dying. When I put her down, she limped back into her den to feel
sorry for herself. I spent most of the night lying on the cement floor with my arm
stretched through the entrance of her den, just touching her gently and trying to
make her feel better.

By this time I too was convinced that she was dying. Tom, however, being much
more realistic than I, was fast asleep in our nice soft waterbed. During the night I
offered her tasty treats, but she was just too injured to eat. So she thought. I gently pulled her out to rest next to me on my pillow but she was still much too weak
to lift her head.

I was determined to get something into her. Finally what saved her life were a few
drops of sugar water. What miraculous healing power the stuff had. She could

actually raise her head now and limp back into her den. By this time the light was beginning to dawn on me. This fox was an actress, Gracie the Klutz alias Gracie the actress.

After the sugar water miracle I decided that it was highly possible that she would live after all. Sleeping on the cement floor was not all that comfortable and I headed for better sleeping quarters. Lo and Behold! Gracie was still alive in the morning, limping, but alive. I'm sure that her leg was sore, but the overacting was a bit ridiculous.

I do not like to raise just one of any kind of animal. I believe that it is much better for them if they have siblings to play and wrestle with. We finally got some good news. A male red fox about the same age as Gracie would be coming to live with us. I thought it was wonderful. Gracie hated him. George was an intruder, a horrible thing. Why did we do this to her? How could we? Get him out of here!

George, on the other hand, was very happy to be somewhere that he had places to hide, mice to catch, things to play with and best of all, a friend.

Gracie would not forgive us. She went back to sulking and hiding. After a few days she began to see George in a different way. George was very persistent about becoming Gracie's friend and she finally started to accept him. He really was kind of fun. He would chase her and they could wrestle and play. Maybe he was okay after all. Soon the two were napping away the daytime, snuggling together and then destroying the greenhouse at night.

Every morning required a major cleanup. I would shovel the piles of dirt back into the orange tree pots, sweep up the feathers from the birdcicle that they played Frisbee with all night, refill the water bowls and locate and arrange toys in a central location. Just so they could do it all again the next night.

Gracie's favorite place to sit was right on top of my head with her front feet planted firmly on my shoulders. She could face either direction, which at times left a large bushy tail hanging between my eyes and spilling over my nose to my neck.

Yet another intruder invaded Gracie's greenhouse. One week before summer vacation our first fawn of the season arrived, a tiny Whitetail doe, a perfect replica of Jessica who had come to us one year ago. We decided to call her J.B. for Jessica's Baby. J.B. lived in the intensive care room that happened to be one of Gracie's favorite places. The room was full of nice fluffy straw in which Gracie loved to burrow. She had to be evicted because J.B. would need the room for a week or so.

The tiny fawn became acquainted with Gracie and didn't seem to mind when she darted in and erased every perfect little nest that she had. When and if you could grab the fox, all the nests had to be rebuilt.

Soon J.B. was visiting the large part of the greenhouse that Gracie eagerly shared with her and two cottontail bunnies and two baby raccoons. The bunnies and raccoons were in cages that doubled as places for Gracie to sleep on or under since her moods changed quite frequently.

As I sat on the floor and held the tiny raccoons and cottontails to bottle feed, J.B. would be exploring and Gracie would be perched on top of my head dusting my face with her tail. Only later in life would the little things that I was holding be threatened by her.

It seems as though I'm always faced with some situation that I worry myself sick over. What would J.B. think of George? Would he chase her and frighten her? I really should not worry as much as I do because there really isn't much that I can do about it anyway. Things usually work themselves out. George and J.B. got along just fine.

It was only the end of May and our menagerie was already growing

7

STARTING ALL OVER AGAIN

The first day of vacation was a very nice uneventful day. J.B. was having short excursions outdoors as were George and Gracie. Jessica came bright and early every day and I marveled at the beautiful yearling doe in her sleek, red, summer coat. She had wintered well and I noticed that her nipples were slightly enlarged. I had never seen a pregnant deer. I didn't know if it were possible for her to be bred before she was one year old. Wouldn't it be incredible if she brought us a fawn?

After two days of vacation things were still quiet. That night, however, about ten o'clock the game warden called. Some campers had a new born bull elk calf stroll into their camp and lie down. Leaving their camp set up they scooped up the thirty pound baby and drove two and a half hours to their home and phoned the officer.

We drove to where the calf was being kept and were escorted through a large barn into a stall where the huge baby calmly bathed in the warmth of a heat lamp. As usual, I was armed with my giant baby bottle full of warm milk. The calf did not seem hungry. He was not dehydrated and seemed very strong. After discussing the situation, we decided that the baby was in good condition and since the campers were returning to their camp it was worth a try to take him back and hopefully his mother would retrieve him.

If things didn't work out, Tom would drive up to their camp early in the morning and if the calf was still there he would bring him home. The drive would take about three and half-hours so Tom left before sunrise.

Tom called me several hours later and informed me that he was headed home and DID NOT have a bull elk. A flood of relief surged through me. I would do everything possible to raise him if I had to, but there is no substitute for a real mother.

Tom arrived home tired from the drive and from walking around searching for signs of the baby elk. About five-thirty that same evening the telephone rang. Thirty minutes after Tom had left guess who came back to camp? This time the campers gave up, packed up their camp and the elk and came home.

The little elk became known as Elmer. Why, I don't really know, he just smiled a lot and looked like his name should be Elmer. Elmer was large enough to be put in the outdoor pen that has a nice warm shelter in the corner. Elmer was as fond of the shelter as Larry had been the previous year. He made short journeys into the pen after feedings. Unlike Larry, who never figured out how to drink from a bottle, Elmer readily took to nursing and was very easy to feed.

J.B. would come to the pen during the day and Jessica would come faithfully every morning and ask permission to enter the pen. Elmer and J.B. would eagerly greet her as she washed and nuzzled them. She would lay down with them for a while and then ask permission again to leave for the day.

Both they and I looked forward to her visits each day. They were giving her all of their affection, which was so much better than having them, imprint on me. Of course I made sure that I got a few ear nibbles also.

Déjà vu, a Whitetail doe and a bull elk calf! The plot thickened. In addition to foxes, deer, elk, squirrels and rabbits we also became the proud owners of nine-teen more baby raccoons. A chimney sweep in a nearby town was getting a fat wallet evicting raccoon families out of perfect little nesting places, chimneys! What a great place to raise a family!

No one in their right mind wants nineteen raccoons and I already had two. The vacant bear cage became the local "coondominium". Who said I was in my right mind anyway?

Young Raccoons

Everything was going quite well. We were busy but not overwhelmed. Jessica's daily visits with Elmer and J.B. were like clockwork. The foxes were getting along beautifully and entertaining themselves. None of the coons had to be bottle fed so they were very easy to care for. They slept all day in a large pile. You couldn't tell whose head belonged to those legs or "Why did that one have a tail sprouting out of the top of its head?" It didn't matter to them. They were very comfortable.

At night the cage exploded with motion. They climbed, they fell, they wrestled and they ate. They ate a lot. One of their favorite times was when I would gather a large jar of grasshoppers and toss them into their cage. Within seconds the hoppers disappeared. The little coons just vacuumed them up.

Raccoons have always amazed me. They never look at what they are fondling. Their eyes are always searching for what they are going to destroy next. None of the raccoons were handled in any way. All they needed was to grow up and be released in good river bottom country.

Father's Day brought Tom something very special. A tiny antelope fawn and a beautiful mule doe fawn. The game warden was going to an exclusive restaurant about thirty miles from us and would deliver them.

I arrived early as usual and as I sat in the parking lot waiting for my new orphans I felt somewhat alien. Why would you want to get all dressed up and waste all that time eating when you could be doing something useful? My summer wardrobe consisted of a pair of cut off jeans, a tee shirt, and a pair of thongs that were not usually on my feet. I don't even own a dress.

When the game warden finally arrived he pulled up next to me, got out and opened the trunk of his car. Right in the middle was a tiny antelope and a tiny mule deer snuggled together. I picked them up as though I was handling the finest china, especially the antelope. She couldn't have weighed more than three or four pounds. She looked like an expensive piece of art that should be put in a glass display case. Antelope are so fragile looking, yet they are one of the hardiest and toughest of all the animals that we handle.

After we gently placed them in my carrier, we headed for home. I was no longer feeling out of place. I had returned to my element.

The little antelope became known as Sugar because she came from a town called Sugar City. The little mule deer was called Millie. I thought back to the days of Dan and Diane and hoped that Sugar would be more cooperative. She was, for awhile!

J.B. was living outdoors full time now with Elmer. The new fawns were put in the intensive care room. They settled down nicely in the straw nests and were fed every four hours.

When we walked into the room, Sugar would look UP her nose at us. Her head was shaped like a light bulb with large protruding black eyes staring at us in amazement. She accepted the bottle easily and would chug her four ounces with gusto. Sometimes she never even bothered to stand up.

After eating, she would stand if she wasn't already standing, position her back legs perfectly and urinate for what seemed like an eternity. I would put a glass under her and she would fill it to the top. If I didn't do this the whole place would have floated away. After this ritual she expected to have her petite little rear end stimulated until she emitted a fragile string of droppings. Then she would return to serious business, rest.

Cecilia & Fawns

Millie on the other hand was not an eager eater. This always bothers me. If they are not willing to eat, it is as though they are giving up. They seem to know that something is wrong.

Millie would hold a bottle in her mouth as I gently massaged her throat to make her swallow. It seemed to take her hours to consume three or four ounces of milk. If that's what it took, that's what we would do. We do not give up!

After a few days with Sugar, I began feeling very smug about owning a nice antelope. Suddenly she started giving me horrified looks when I entered the room to feed her. I had turned into some kind of monster. She would bolt away from me and literally run up the walls. I would sit quietly and try to calm her but something about me had changed and she no longer trusted me. I was afraid that she was going to kill herself. For some unknown reason she still trusted Tom, so he took over the task of feeding her.

Millie was getting weaker. Her will to live was slowly slipping from her frail spotted little body. There was nothing that I could do. Did Sugar think that I had something to do with this? Was she afraid that I would do the same thing to her?

After ten days Millie left us. Her death left Sugar more terrified of me than before. Millie died with me lying next to her in her bed of straw in the intensive care room. It is so difficult to want to help them and know that it is not in your hands anymore. Her life may have been short but she left a part of herself behind as so many others have a memory.

I promptly removed Millie from the room and Sugar was left alone. Her constant companion for the last ten days was gone. Did she blame me? I wanted so badly to comfort her and explain to her, but she wanted no part of me.

When Tom went in to feed her, I sneaked in as unobtrusively as possible and tried to gain back her trust. I crouched in the corner enviously as she took her bottle from Tom and then danced around him and showed off until she tired and returned to her bed.

I was afraid to move her to the outdoor pen. If she could do forty-five miles an hour inside what would she do in a large area?

A few days later a little doe was brought to us by someone who had found her along side a road on a very hot day. Sugar's reaction to the new fawn was much to my delight. I had returned her friend. She instantly welcomed the new little fawn and bedded down with her.

At the 10:00 p.m. feeding the little doe was extremely feverish. She was so hot that she was panting and very weak. We immediately wrapped her in cold towels to bring her temperature down. Within an hour she seemed normal and I left the two and went to bed.

In the morning when I went into the room to feed at five o'clock I found that the little doe had died in her sleep. Sugar was alone again. I couldn't take another friend from Sugar. We would just have to take our chances and introduce her to the outdoor group.

Tom covered her with a large towel, got a secure grip on her and carried her to the pen. With hearts pounding we waited for the explosion. When she was unveiled we were greatly relieved when she just stood there. She carefully scrutinized the scene and seemed to be saying "What took you so long to get me out here?" Her introduction to Jess, J.B., and Elmer went smoothly and once more Sugar had friends. I was okay again and she trusted me enough to feed her.

Just a few days before Sugars' big move outdoors we were confronted with yet another sad situation. Sunday morning our game warden brought up a little mule buck fawn. The night before his right front leg had been severed right below the knee by a hay-mowing machine. He also had deep lacerations on his sides and head.

We simply called him Little Buck. We had to give him a chance. He did not seem to be in pain. We cleaned and dressed the wounds as best as we could and called the vet.

When an animal is injured as severely as he was, stress is the biggest factor in determining whether they will pull through or not. In a few days, after he got some rest and nourishment we would take him to the vet for a complete amputation.

He enjoyed the company of the others in the pen and could get around very well on his three good legs. He would not take the bottle very well so we tube fed him three times a day. After his feedings he would lie in my arms and nuzzle my ears and neck. He too looked forward to Jessica's daily visits. Jess was very gentle with him. She knew that he needed extra attention and the two of us gave it to him.

8

HAPPY BIRTHDAY

On July tenth while doing all of my early morning chores, I saw Jessica in the scrub oak on the other side of the yard. She did not make her appearance in the pen that morning. Jessica, having a mind of her own probably just didn't feel like it.

Late that evening after J.B., Elmer, and Sugar were fed I was sitting in the middle of the pen with Little Buck. Suddenly the three rushed to the corner of the pen and were very excited. I stood up to see what they were so anxious about and saw Jessica staring back at them.

Jess seemed very agitated. She stood with her ears pricked forward, neck arched and head held high. She then snorted loudly sending the three little ones off in a panic. J.B. ran into the fence and fell down, Elmer bolted for the shelter and I yelled for Tom. He had gone into the house to wash the bottles and finally heard me calling.

As Jessica turned to leave, I could see that her rear end was swollen and bloody. Tom came out to see what was going on and I stayed in the pen cradling Little Buck and soothing the others. I heard Tom talking softly to Jessica while he approached her. From where I was sitting, the shelter blocked my view. After a few minutes I heard Tom say in a very excited but soft tone "Cec, Jess has a baby!"

By this time everyone in the pen had calmed down and I went out to where Jessica was proudly showing Tom her fawn. About thirty feet from the pen lying in the tall grass under a Russian Olive tree was our grandchild. The baby was camouflaged so well that Jess had to poke and prod Tom several times while trying to show him where it was. He was practically standing on top of it. Jessica was very proud of her baby.

What an incredible day! Most fawns are born in May and June. Jess must have been bred late since she was so young, but she obviously had no problems and seemed to know exactly what she was doing.

After showing off her baby, Jess insisted on her visit to the pen to see the orphans. She washed them, ate with them, lay down for awhile and then asked to leave. She put her fawn in a safe place and left for the night.

We knew exactly where the baby was but never went back to see it. We did not want to disturb it or interfere in any way. Maybe we could learn something about how real deer raise their young by watching Jessica and her fawn.

Gracie and George were now living outdoors full time. They never walked anywhere. They raced. They slept the day away in the scrub oak behind the deer pen and at night they did what foxes are supposed to do, terrorize everything!

We sleep outdoors most of the summer on a rollaway bed on our deck overlooking the deer pen. George never bothered us at night, but Gracie was downright obnoxious. Sometimes she snuggled on Tom's pillow or on his chest. Other times she would race full speed down the twenty-five foot long deck and fly onto the bed using our heads as a springboard to leap onto the ground and into the bushes. If you wiggled your toes under the blankets she would sit up as straight as she could, cock her head from side to side and then leap straight up and then down, face first onto her prey, (your big toe).

Things were quite tense that night because we knew Jessica's baby was sleeping less than fifty feet from us. Jessica had told her baby to stay put. I found it very difficult to relax knowing that the two maniac foxes were running rampant so close to where the fawn was. The two never bothered her during the night. It wasn't our business any way. It is difficult to not want to interfere. We were positive that Jessica knew what she was doing and trusted her judgment completely.

The next morning when I awoke about an hour before sunrise, I sat up in bed and the first thing I saw was my beautiful Jessica nursing her own fragile fawn. How special it was to be witnessing such a beautiful sight. She then moved the baby into the nearby scrub, put it to bed and came to visit the orphans.

Jessica & Josie

The next week passed and we only saw the baby from a distance. Jess was not ready to introduce her fawn to her orphan friends. Jessica kept in constant contact with her fawn by using a very low throaty sound. It reminded me of the sounds that whales use to communicate. The sound must have been able to carry a long distance.

During the excitement of watching Jessica in her new found motherhood, our little buck was still not nursing. He had made it through major surgery, having his front leg completely amputated at the shoulder, and seemed fine except for not wanting to nurse by himself. Every feeding was through a tube.

One evening while feeding him I noticed that he had a very difficult time trying to stand, his stomach was severely distended. Our vet said to bring him to the clinic right away. The little buck again went through surgery to try to correct a hernia that was a result of his original injuries.

After a two hour operation, the little buck died before he came out of the anesthetic. His short stay with us was an inspiration to everyone who knew him. They give so much more than they ask for.

After the morning feeding J.B., Elmer, and Sugar were now allowed to leave the pen and explore a larger environment. When Jessica's fawn was about two weeks old, she felt that it was time to introduce it to her instant family. While the baby was around, we were very careful not to interfere or get too close. We just sat back and enjoyed watching the family get to know each other.

George and Gracie were very curious about the newcomer. They teased and played but never with any intent to harm. Perhaps it was her relationship with Larry that surfaced when Jessica thought Elmer was getting a bit rough. She was not real fond of the big baby being too close to hers.

In mid July we received another whitetail doe. We called her Jane Doe. Jane was taken away from a family and we hoped that she was not too severely imprinted on people. She was older than any of our fawns and very independent.

The game warden that brought her to us didn't bother to put her in a carrier. He simply placed her on the front seat of his truck. Janey didn't like the idea and proceeded to kick out his windshield. She got some good licks in on him, too. After the embarrassing ordeal he decided to blindfold and hobble her.

When the officer handed her over to Tom, things went a lot smoother. He, in his gentle manner, calmly placed her in our large pet carrier, covered it to make it dark, and the rest of the journey home was incident free.

One look at Jessica, and Jane Doe was convinced that she had found her mother. Jessica adopted her just as she had the other fawns.

One beautiful Sunday morning as I was feeding, I noticed that Elmer was not interested in his bottle. He usually was the pushiest one of the bunch and the one who took the most milk. He ignored the bottle and went into the brush and lay down. My spirits plummeted. He was running a temperature so we immediately put him on antibiotics and left him to rest.

I was encouraged that evening when he came to feed but not with his usual gusto. At least he took some milk and it did make me feel better. The next morning he again ate but was obviously not much better than the day before. The usual light-heartedness of feeding time turned ominous. While the others played, Elmer just returned to his shelter.

I need to be near them when they are ill. Just being close to them and letting them know that they are not alone seems to help. That night I slept in the shelter with him. It had been raining all day but the shelter was warm and dry. About midnight Elmer got up and nuzzled me and seemed to be feeling better. Then he walked out into the pen and was looking for something to eat.

I felt relieved and watched him move around the pen. After a few minutes I noticed that he was walking the same pattern as if he didn't know where he was. I herded him back into the shelter and wrestled with him until he lay down. Within minutes he was up again standing as close to the wall as he could get and shoving up against it. He would then walk in a tight circle always going in the same direction. What was happening to Elmer?

After about an hour of this he seemed to tire out and finally settled down into a deep sleep. By this time I was soaking wet from the constant drizzle and was freezing. I decided to go inside to warm up and try to get some sleep. It was after one o'clock when I fell asleep.

About four o'clock I went out to check on Elmer. He had come out of the shelter sometime during the night, found his way to the corner of the pen and must have walked in circles the rest of the night.

He had walked the same pattern repeatedly, each time rubbing against the chain link fence. The hair on his forehead and chest had been completely rubbed off leaving his exposed skin bloody and raw. He had no idea where he was. I was sick. Here was my happy little elk who loved to be clean and always well groomed.

We suspected a virus had attacked his central nervous system. Our vet suggested a tranquilizer to keep him calm. With a sedative he hopefully would stay quiet. The tranquilizer would only keep him down for thirty or forty minutes and then he was up circling and thrashing again.

I spent the next two nights in the shelter with him but I was losing hope. We were giving him a chance but the medication did not seem to be doing anything for him. We would have to make a decision soon. This really wasn't fair to him. I desperately wanted to see some improvement. We would give him one more day. Our beautiful smiling little elk was no longer the same. A vicious virus was devouring his mind.

The next day I had to drive about seventy miles to pick up another whitetail fawn. Tom stayed home with the little bit of hope that we still had for Elmer. Jessica came that morning and paid her last respects. She sensed our sorrow and in her own special way said goodbye to Elmer.

With a mixed feeling of sorrow and joy, I left to pick up the new fawn. At last, a whitetail buck, a perfect addition for Jessica's collection. On the return trip my thoughts turned again to what I would have to face when we arrived at home.

Elmer was worse. The sedative would not keep him down at all. He came out of his shelter and fell to the ground. I too, went down with him and held him as Tom administered a shot that would release him from his agony. He could finally rest. Maybe we could get some rest too. The last few days were physically and mentally draining. Elmer was gone now, but his spirit will always be here.

His life had a strange beginning and I am confident that the time he spent with us was a very happy time for him. It certainly was for us. In his few short weeks he had experienced lots of friends, a chance to be free and tons of love. They always seem to give so much yet ask so little in return. Life is for the living and we certainly had plenty of living things that required our attention.

The confident new little buck was placed in the deer pen to familiarize himself with his new environment. Sugar, J.B. and Jane were out for the day with Jess and her baby when he arrived. That evening when the group came home, the little guy attacked Jessica and tried to nurse. She wouldn't let him so he gave up and took a bottle from me.

The family left and the little buck stayed in the pen his first night. In the morning he again tried to get breakfast from Jess and once again she shoved him off. At least he knew that I was available with the bottle when this happened.

Jessica and her family were out all the time now. The little ones were no longer confined to the pen at night. I thought it would be best to keep the new fawn in the pen a few days to get acquainted with his new surroundings.

In the morning, after the family left for the day, I let him out to explore. He immediately took off and headed straight for a neighbor's house. I followed him and tried to catch him but he ditched me by ducking into the scrub oak. I gave up and returned home.

The last few days were very stressful and now I was even more frustrated. Walking home taking giant strides I muttered to myself, "Who does this little guy think he is anyway? Why can't he cooperate? Everyone else is. What a big shot. Let him go! I don't care!"

Fifteen minutes later I decided to go looking for him. I put the carrier in my car and was determined to find him and bring him home, the little brat.

As I drove slowly down the road scanning and searching for him, I saw the cocky little buck march across the road right in front of me. His head was held high and his white tail flagged. I decided not to chase him. I knew that I couldn't catch him anyway. I parked the truck and followed him on foot. He acted as though he knew exactly what he was doing and where he was going.

He made a large loop through the pasture across the road and then proceeded to head up the mountain. I then lost sight of him and decided that I should warn the summer visitors at the cabin near our house. They had two dogs with them that would certainly give chase if they saw the little deer. They quickly put the dogs in a pen and we sat outside the cabin watching and visiting.

A short time later the little fawn strutted past us as though he were a five point buck. He crossed through the wire fence into the llama pasture, passed through the fence on the other side, and went through our front yard directly into the deer pen. He recognized it as home and was confident enough to find his way there. Definitely a high I.Q. little buck. I can still see him strutting through the pasture, giving the llamas looks that seemed to say, "I dare you." Boy was I relieved.

After this exploration of his new world, the confident little buck became known as "Marco Polo". Marco was now a part of Jessica's family. After a few days he even convinced her that she had enough milk for him too. He stayed closer to her than her real baby who hadn't been named yet because we didn't know if it was a buck or a doe.

About two weeks later we finally determined that Jessica's fawn was a doe. One day the opportunity arose to watch closely as the little one urinated. Jessica's baby was named "Josie". Jessica is a whitetail and her fawn's father had to be a mule deer. We had an outlaw deer, The Outlaw Josie Whitetails. If the fawn had been a buck we were going to call him Jesse's James.

Josie never did trust us nor did we encourage her to do so. She was always with Jess and the others as we fed and touched them for various reasons. She would just look at them as though they were crazy to associate with us.

Marco never missed an opportunity to nurse from Jess. When Josie was hungry, she and Marco would race to Jessica who would proudly stand braced for all the punching and shoving until they satisfied themselves. If she thought they had enough before they did, she would just climb off them. What a saint she was!

9

HERE COME THE BEARS

As the month of August was unraveling we somberly waited for the day that we had to return to our jobs. Things were going beautifully. Each morning was such a joy to witness. The days were filled with chores and the evenings were peaceful. Marco was the last arrival and he now was in Jessica's hands, or should I say hooves.

Again the serenity was broken. A mother bear had been killed on a highway leaving behind two orphaned cubs. That evening the two arrived along with a little mule deer fawn that had been taken away from a sheepherder. The little fawn had been living in an overturned stock tank.

Our bear cage was overflowing with raccoons and we had no choice but to keep the cubs in the den of the cage until the coons could be shipped off. It was time for them to leave. We had just been putting it off since things were going so smoothly.

The little buck was put in the deer pen until he could meet his new family. The little orphan bears were put in the den, fed and left alone so that they could finally get some rest and settle in. The next morning was something I was not looking forward to. I had to catch all those raccoons without getting shredded. No wonder we put it off!

Wearing thick padded gloves up to my elbows I began plucking and pulling them off the perches, off the sides of the cage and out of their dens. They were like Velcro strips. I can still hear the noises coming out of that cage. Tom stood next to me holding our largest pet carrier. I would snag a coon and he would open the door. When I dropped it in, he would quickly close it as I went after another.

When the last coon was deposited in the carrier, the silence was almost deafening. What an accomplishment! We had all the raccoons in the carrier and I had not lost one drop of blood.

Our release area for raccoons is only about fifteen miles from where we live. The drive was extremely quiet. The raccoons seemed to know that they were returning to their real world. It is such a pleasure to give them what they deserve.

The area was raccoon heaven, countless trees to climb and nest in and acres and acres of wonderful things to examine with their incredible little hands. They were excited to get out of their jail and begin a new life. We wished them well and returned home to scour their cage and prepare it for the bear cubs.

The cubs spent only three weeks with us and then were released with a foster mother who was being relocated. The past year had been very hot and dry. Conditions for bears were very poor. The wild plums and acorns, major food sources, were nonexistent. These conditions forced the bears to move in closer to humans in search of food. Since most people are not thrilled about having a bear rummage through their trash looking for food, the bears had to be trapped and moved.

Two days after the release of the cubs yet another pair of orphan bears were entertaining the people of a city about twenty miles north of us. They were trying to locate food by themselves and no one knew what had happened to their mother. The first of the two was captured by a dog catcher and then taken to the local animal shelter. The shelter then called the wildlife officer who told them to call us.

Tom is becoming quite famous at the animal shelter. His patience in dealing with problem animals is miraculous. While everyone else is freaking out and in a panic, he calmly handles the situation with as little stress as possible to the animal involved.

One day he was called to the shelter to pick up an adult raccoon that had been raiding trash cans. The coon was trapped and brought to the shelter by the irate homeowner. Wild adult raccoons are not the easiest animal to handle. In an attempt to get the coon into a carrier the caretaker accidentally let the animal escape from the cage it had been brought in.

The raccoon raced into the kitchen area and was running up and down the racks containing large metal feeding pans, bouncing them off the walls, the floor and the people who were standing and watching in amazement.

After all of the people had left the room screaming, Tom followed the coon, cornered him, noose poled him and brought him home. The unhappy raccoon was given his freedom the same day in a wildlife area void of trash cans and humans.

Tom went to the animal shelter to pick up the orphan bear cub. The thirty pound cub was in the process of reshaping the dilapidated coyote trap that had captured him. The little bear was at the rear of the eight foot long trap and had managed to pull the door inside with him making it impossible to open. Tom had to kick the door so it would move freely and then crawl in, face to face with the unhappy little cub. His only weapon was a noose pole. He successfully caught him and dragged him out and transferred him into a carrier. Again Tom was the hero of the animal shelter.

Boris

Our new little bear seemed very content with his food supply and living quarters. I knew that his brother was still at large and that it would only be a matter of time before he too joined us. I was right. On a September Sunday morning the little cub was climbing trees in front of the state prison on the busiest street through town. His antics in the treetops had successfully stopped two bus loads of Japanese tourists and several cars.

It was a very tense situation as the crowd gathered to watch the game wardens rescue the little guy. He had to be shot with a tranquilizer dart because he was too high up in the tree to be reached by climbing. As the little body tumbled to the safety of the stretched tarp spread for him, the silence was broken by cheers and clapping from the onlookers. The relieved crowd broke up and the little cub was brought to live with his sibling.

Two days later the cubs got more company. Two more orphan cubs. Four bear cubs can consume a lot of food! A local orchard donated all the apples that the four could eat. A fifty pound bag of Puppy Chow lasted two days. With a bear's ability to store fat, it did not take long for their thin little bodies to fill out with the much needed fat that would take them through the winter.

Three and a half weeks later two of the cubs were released with another foster mother and a week after that the other two left with a mother bear that had her own cub. Our orphaned cubs were introduced to their foster mothers in an experimental way. The new mothers were tranquilized and their noses were then packed with Vicks Vaporub. The Vicks kept the mother from being able to distinguish the orphans as strangers.

This method seemed very effective. When the cubs were released with their new mother they romped off after her as if they had known her all their lives. It was an experiment, but at least it gave them a second chance for surviving the coming winter.

The middle of October seemed to bring to an end the arrival of the year's orphans. Jessica and her family were doing remarkably well. All of the fawns were now out of spots and sporting thick winter coats. Every evening the group would parade through the llama pasture and into the yard for their free meal.

Each year I have someone who is very difficult to wean. This year it was Sugar. The little antelope insisted on having her bottle at least once a day. As the others feasted on grain and hay, Sugar would stand at the door and lick her lips until I went out with the large bottle of watered down milk.

Most of the time when deer cut through the llama pasture, the llamas would just ignore them. Occasionally Parika would give chase. The whitetails would just flag their tails and jump over or go through the fence, but Sugar would remain for a contest with him.

Her speed was incredible and as Parika would gain on her she would kick into high gear, make a hair pin turn and zing by him going the opposite way. By the time he realized what had happened she would be long gone.

The little orphan mule buck that arrived with the two bear cubs only stayed with Jessica's family for a few days. He found his place with the mule deer in the area. A doe with twins finally adopted him. The little guy was so pushy that I'm sure that she didn't have much choice.

Gracie and George were young adults by now. Gracie was still her obnoxious self and I saw her every morning and every evening. George had gotten very elusive and we rarely saw him

10

THE YEAR COMES TO AN END

October and November bring the hunting season. We have a difficult time dealing with this time of the year. Our two bucks Tim and Tim were very vulnerable this year. Both were sporting beautiful three point racks. Although we know that we can't protect them it is difficult not to want to. We raise them to be what they should be and hunting is part of the game. I would, however, prefer not to be a witness.

I live for the hunting season to be over. Each day a large black X is marked on the calendar. I breathed a sigh of relief on the night of the last day of the season. That night I watched from the bedroom window. The bucks were dozing in the full moonlight with their does and fawns. Perhaps they would be blessed with yet another year of precious life. They were truly magnificent.

Surely the year was over! Not so. November fifteenth brought us another hungry black bear cub. He had been captured in a corn field two weeks earlier and moved to a remote area with better bear accommodations. In one week the little cub had traveled over fifty miles and had gotten himself into another jam. This time he was brought to us.

The game warden brought him to our house in a bear trap and left him in the barn until we got home from work. A little note was attached to the trap saying, "Tom and Cec, this one needs some extra TLC." The little cub was nothing but skin and bones. His fur was matted with cockleburs and he was now sporting two yellow ear tags from his first encounter with man. It was much too late in the year to fatten him up and relocate him. He would be with us until spring.

TLC he got, plenty of it. He was given a warm, cozy den loaded with straw and tons of good food. In no time at all he was on the road to recovery. "Bobo" was a very lucky little bear.

Thanksgiving was upon us and again we had plenty to be thankful for. The day was shared by the friends that we are the closest to: Our mothers and all of our foster children. Our dinner was shared by everyone. The turkey carcass was finished by the skunks, magpies, and crows. The only thing that I had to throw away was the aluminum pan that it was prepared in.

The time between Thanksgiving and Christmas is hectic for everyone. As I baked and shopped, my thoughts returned to Christmas one year ago when we lost our llama "Briggs". Our family had certainly grown since then and I again cherished my memories and looked forward to our two week vacation.

I will never forget the day that we got our Christmas tree. A real tree is the best part of Christmas. I can't make myself cut one but we always purchase one. Jessica's family was in the yard when we arrived home with our tree. As I carried the heavy tree to the deck, each of them came to inspect and admire it. I can't begin to express the beauty of that moment. They seemed to think that I did a good job in selecting such a gorgeous and tasty tree.

Soon they would be admiring the tree as it proudly displayed its many colorful lights and decorations in front of the windows of our living room. Not only Jessica's family, but the whole mule deer herd enjoyed the tree we decorated for them.

Christmas also brought us "Gramps". One night a few days before Christmas I looked out at the herd of deer gathered in the yard. In front of a pinion tree about twenty feet from the house lay a large mule deer. He was sound asleep, his large mule ears drooped on the snow. His antlers were gnarled and stubby. He looked so weak that I was afraid that I would find him dead in the morning.

He was obviously very old. The does and fawns had introduced him to our yard and I believe that coming here night after night through the winter gave Gramps a whole new outlook on life. He must have been a wise old man to have survived this long. Large bucks are a real prize during hunting season.

Gramps became a nightly visitor to our yard. Within a few weeks he had gained weight and we watched him frolic with the fawns and flirt with the does. It was obvious that he was the oldest member of the herd and still had the respect of the larger bucks. Gramps deserved a retirement home.

On Christmas morning Jessica and her family were feasting on hay and grain. It was her second Christmas with us. Would she ever leave us? When they finished and were leaving through the pasture, I noticed that Sugar was limping on her right back leg. Her little ankle was slightly swollen but she was determined to follow her friends. She trailed after them to spend her first Christmas on the sunny hillside about a half a mile from our house.

At two o'clock that afternoon Sugar limped home and positioned herself in the middle of the alfalfa hay pile and rested until the rest of the herd came home in the evening. I couldn't help but notice that she limped more obviously when I was watching.

Sugar was a strange addition to the whitetail family, but they accepted her as though she were one of them. Other antelope that we have raised have always been moved to other locations. I hated to move Sugar. We were not that far from antelope country and if she ever decided to leave she would not have that far to go. Sugar was happy;

Sugar was free. What difference did it make where she was? She knew what she was.

When the deer cross a fence they either jump over or climb through. Sugar's true antelope behavior would take over and she would get down on her knees and crawl under the bottom wire. Her curiosity left her staring at things that sent the deer running. Only after she studied something intently did she decide if it were necessary to expend the energy to leave. If she decided that the situation was too dangerous to stick around, however, the stiff legged little bundle of energy would explode and disappear.

One day while Sugar was basking in the winter sun, four wild turkeys strutted into the yard. Sugar stood up, flared her rump and was on her way. Suddenly she came to an abrupt stop and turned to face the turkeys and get a better look. She wasn't quite sure. How dangerous were they? I better go! No, wait a minute.

After several stop and go attempts Sugar decided that they really were dangerous after all, definitely a threat to her safety. Within thirty seconds she disappeared over the crest of a hill almost half a mile away.

Bobo the black bear was dozing and eating himself back to health. We should have named him Grumpy. His attitude was not all that pleasant. We laughed as he huffed and puffed when we walked by his cage.

A few weeks before Christmas we received word of another black bear cub who had been stealing dog food from a cattle ranchers' dog. The game warden had set the trap time after time but the little cub was too light to trigger it and catch himself. It was late December and the starving cub couldn't possibly survive the winter. Just a few days after Christmas, he was finally captured.

I thought Bobo would be thrilled to have company, but to my dismay, the two could not tolerate each other. Unfortunately, the cage that we have has only one den and the fat Bobo occupied it and was not going to share it with anyone. I made a makeshift den in the opposite corner of the cage and we got along quite well.

With someone else sharing his living quarters, Bobo got very selfish. He now thought that all the bowls were his and would drag them into his den. I had to retrieve them with a hoe and would experience a tug of war with him each time I tried to get them.

Surely within a few days they would become acquainted and realize that there was room and food enough for the two of them. The new cub, which we named Bubu, had her corner, Bobo had his den and all of my bowls, and I had my hoe. We managed.

Toward the end of January Bubu inched her way closer to the den and they actually shared the large food bowl. Occasionally she would try to sneak into the den only to cause a terrible vocal disagreement. Bobo always won.

One afternoon about mid February I was moving some large unsplit pine logs from the wood pile and had to roll them past their cage. The first huge log that I rolled by scared the daylights out of Bubu and she charged into the den. Bobo or no Bobo she was more frightened of the rolling log than she was of the fat troll who was selfishly controlling the den. After some serious bear conversation, which sounded rather bossy to me, Bobo's fat body emerged from the den and Bubu was now in control.

Bobo was not very happy about the new arrangement and let us know by whining, complaining, and pouting. I had no idea that a bear could make such pitiful sounds. "Fluf, fluf, fluf, fluf, please let me in fluf, fluf, fluf."

That night as Bubu contentedly slept inside the den, Bobo slept right outside. She was kind enough to let him rest his head inside the entryway. The roles had reversed. I hadn't realized until this time that he was actually afraid of her.

Gradually the two decided that they were both bears and there was plenty of food. They could both fit in the den comfortably, so "What the heck, let's be friends."

It certainly made life a lot easier for me. I had to smile every time I passed by their cage. Instead of all the huffing and puffing and fluffing, they would be gently playing or snoring soundly, snuggled together, patiently waiting for spring.

11

SPRING COMES AGAIN

Spring was returning to the mountain. The late winter storms move through quickly, leaving wet snow to tempt the grasses to poke through the muddy earth. The deer were still coming to the yard twice a day for short visits. Each morning I looked forward to seeing the five whitetails and Sugar.

Early in March the family came one morning, but there were only four whitetails and Sugar.

Marco, the little buck was not with them. I didn't think too much about it since it was the time of year when they start to go off on their own. He was probably somewhere with some bucks his own size. He would be back. In the evening, Marco did not show up again.

For the next ten days I eagerly waited for their arrival to see if Marco had returned. My heart sank each time I only counted four deer. After dark I would peer out the windows to see if I could spot the little whitetail with the mule deer that usually came after sundown. Marco was not with them.

I thought back to the time of Marco's arrival. He was an adventurer. I decided that the urge had hit him to go on another excursion. I would see him again. I had that feeling. I just wanted to get a glimpse of him to be sure that he was all right. I knew Marco was a very intelligent little buck. He had proved that the first few days that he was with us. Still, I worried.

Every day I would ask Jessica to please bring Marco home. She would roll her beautiful brown eyes and nuzzle my ears and face, convincing me that she knew where he was and when the time was right, he would come back. "If you don't bring him home Jess, at least tell him that I love him."

On the evening of Saint Patrick's Day we were driving out of the yard as the Whitetails and Sugar were coming through the fence into the yard. We got out of the car to greet them. There were five whitetails and Sugar. Marco had come home!

He was as eager to see us as we were to see him. He trotted over and greeted us. I ran inside to get him some of his favorite snacks, grapes and apples. As he was devouring the food I examined him and found a large cut on his front leg. The cut was already healing, so it must have been the reason that we had not seen him for eleven days.

Jessica glanced over her shoulder with a twinkle in her eye. When it was time to bring Marco home, she would bring him, and she did! Where had he been? Did Jess really know where he was? What happened to his leg? These are questions to which I will never know the answers. I can only be thankful to be a part of the little miracles that occurred every day.

Marco was home, he was well. That is all that mattered. I have no control over their lives, just the special privilege to be a part of them. What would the coming spring bring?

Gracie was still coming to visit her treat bowl after dark. She would no longer come if we were outside. We only caught glimpses of her through the window as she leaped up and took one thing at a time out of her bowl. Gracie loved eggs. I would hate to guess the number of raw eggs that we gave her.

Lee, a good friend of mine, was very fond of Gracie. On Easter Sunday, Lee had brought a specially decorated egg to put in her bowl. The egg was brightly colored and covered with shiny sequins. After examining the egg to make sure that nothing on it could harm her if she ate it, we placed it in her bowl and went inside to wait for her to come. Sure enough the glittering egg was the first to disappear.

Gracie

A week later we were taking the llamas for a walk. As we slowly walked up the road I noticed something out of place. There really should be nothing unusual about fox scat. The one that caught my eye however was adorned with a pink heart-shape sequin, a gift from our crazy, clumsy fox, Gracie. I will always treasure this little gift. After all, how many people have a rhinestone fox scat?

12

THE WHITETAIL EXODUS

Jessica and her family were not spending much time in the yard during April. All the new grass and budding trees kept them on the move.

The last day of April surprised everyone. We awoke that morning to eighteen inches of beautiful wet snow. It snowed every day the first week of May. When it was all over, we had received over forty inches. This, of course, sent the entire mule deer herd and Jessica's family back to the security of their winter feeding ground, our yard.

The bear cubs, Bobo and Bubu, were to leave us on May fourth, but their departure was delayed until the following week because of the heavy snowstorm. By Sunday morning, May the sixth, all of the snow had seeped into the ground and left things more beautiful than ever. That morning I saw Sugar momentarily as she passed through the yard. In the evening everyone was there as usual.

Arrangements were made to release the bear cubs Friday, May eleventh. Our thoughts turned to preparing for their release. My evenings were spent picking luscious dandelions in the nearby alfalfa fields. The two cubs would gorge themselves on the plants. They were also eating piles of young grasses. I wanted them to eat as much natural food as possible before they left.

The whitetail family was not coming at all. I assumed that Jessica had her new fawn and was just staying hidden. More than a week had passed since I had seen them.

A few days later, my friend Lee called. She is the secretary at the Wildlife Office. While she was visiting with a fisherman who had come into the office, he made the comment that the weekend before he had seen the "damnedest" thing. About twelve miles from where we live, the fisherman had seen nine whitetail deer crossing the highway toward the river bottom. Not really so strange. Stuck to the herd of deer like glue, however, was a scruffy little antelope.

Lee simply made the comment that it must have been quite a sight. She didn't tell him that she knew six of them by name. As soon as the fisherman left, Lee called and gave me the news. No wonder I hadn't seen them. I was in total shock! Somewhere in the back of my mind I had wondered if they would ever leave our area.

The family had followed Hardscrabble Creek, which is about one and a half miles from our house. Hardscrabble empties into the Arkansas River, whitetail country. Somewhere along their travels they had picked up four more whitetail deer.

What a miracle! We had raised Jessica from practically a newborn. She had helped Larry, her elk friend, find his place and then stayed with us long enough to assemble a herd of her own kind and then migrate to a country more suitable for her species. I missed her and her group terribly. My dreams of her helping this coming spring with our new orphans vanished as quickly as she did.

Their journey also took Sugar to antelope country. I envied them for weeks, pitied myself, but envied them. They simply chose to move. She didn't have to sell her house or worry about insurance or retirement. They were here one day and gone forever the next. The last day that we saw them was May sixth, which also happens to be our anniversary, a date that I will never forget.

My thoughts returned to about a year before the family left us. I was sitting out in the llama pasture after a spring shower. A double rainbow in the east framed the world in which I was sitting. The wild flowers and the new waxy leaves of the scrub oak glistened with the raindrops on them. The silence was broken by a sound behind me and as I turned I saw Jessica jump the fence and come to me.

The two of us shared the moment in silence. Her eyes had a certain beauty in them that reflected the incredible creature that she was. She always had a few nibbles and licks to show her love.

Jessica was magical. Everything about her was slightly unreal. She had spent two years with us. Two years that will never be forgotten. Now, after not seeing her, I wonder if it all really did happen. Somehow, deep inside, I feel that we will see her again. Maybe it is only because I want to so badly. I felt such emptiness without her magical presence. I couldn't wait to see her new baby.

Whitetails, with good nutrition can easily have triplets. Knowing the amount of food she and her family consumed in our yard during the winter, Jessica would surely have a litter. I could see it now. I would be famous. "Whitetail doe gives birth to eight healthy fawns! Five bucks and three does! Rehabilitator takes credit…!"

During the cold winter months when natural foods were scarce and the wild deer came to the yard to feed, Jessica made sure that her group ate first, pinning her ears back and chasing the mule deer off until her family was full. Even little Marco would threaten the bucks that were twice his size. He was proving that he could protect his does.

Janey looked as though she was going to have a fawn this spring also. She always had a big sister attitude toward J.B. They were like a couple of teenage sisters. Josie, Jessica's real baby, after seeing me daily for nine months, still had no use for me. I loved that quality in her. How did she know that she shouldn't trust me although everyone else in the herd did?

One morning Josie and Janey were on the deck raiding the bird feeder as I came out the door and startled them. Josie wasn't taking any chances. One look at me and she launched herself over the two foot wall and sailed to safety seven feet below. Just can't trust those humans!

Then there was Sugar, my little space alien, whom they all hovered over and took care of although she was weird and liked to flip out occasionally and ram into them for no apparent reason.

From a standing position, Sugar could begin a spinning, twirling routine that would put any gymnast to shame. When she was tiny she would drink muddy water then look up at you with perfectly shaped mud lips, and blink her gigantic black eyes. She was the "neutral" between Jessica's whitetails and the mule deer. Everybody liked Shuggy.

The day after I heard about the great exodus I received a call from a friend. He wanted to know if we got the little antelope that was seen in a hayfield. The hayfield just happened to be near the place where the fisherman saw the herd crossing the highway.

Sugar managed to get her picture in the Canon City "Daily Record" newspaper. She was just taking advantage of the luscious hay and the land owner was concerned for her safety.

I got the name and phone number of the man who reported her to the Division of Wildlife and the newspaper and called him immediately and explained her presence. He was very supportive and was only interested in her safety. Also seen in the area were, "of all things" whitetail deer!

Sugar's newly acquired homestead was that of Mr. Bill Shade, who has since become a friend and has graciously offered his acreage along the river bottom as a release area for our orphan raccoons and opossums. Mr. Shade has called us after three more sightings of Sugar, the last being in the fall of the year.

Sugar

Deep down I wanted them to come home again, maybe in the winter when things got tough and food was scarce. On the realistic side, however, I knew that it would be best if we never saw them again. At the time I was suffering the empty nest syndrome. What I really needed were some new orphans to fill the vacancy in my life. That would happen soon enough. Maybe I should have enjoyed the lull.

13

WHERE THE DEER AND THE ANTELOPE PLAY

The next year would prove to be our most stressful. If someone had predicted the events of the oncoming year I would have chosen not to participate.

The spring of 1990 started at the usual pace. Two baby opossums had been spared after their mother and two siblings were killed by a car. Although they were quite small they were able to eat on their own. They were no problem to keep.

The most charming creature of the year was "Sweet Potato", a tennis ball sized beaver that was transferred to us after being found on the main street of a nearby town. She was probably the victim of a non-thinking human who stole her from her lodge and then abandoned her. Some "humans?" think this is a cute thing to do.

I called her a "her" just because she seemed like a "her". Tom said it was a female because she complained a lot. Her biggest complaint was having her pudgy little face wiped clean after her baby cereal feeding. She would double up her front feet into tight little fists, try to hide her face and gripe the whole time I wiped her clean with a warm wet towel. It really couldn't have been that bad.

Sweet Potato

Beaver are difficult to sex because their sex organs are hidden inside an opening called a cloaca. It really didn't matter what sex she was. The joy that she shared with us for two months was deeply felt. Memories of Sweet Potato bring nothing but smiles.

Our first day of vacation was spent doing things that we had put off for the last week. Our refrigerator had finally burned out so it along with the clothes dryer was hauled off. The refrigerator went to the dump and the dryer to the repair shop. My trusty Bronco also had to be taken in for repairs that would take at least three days. I was relieved that they had agreed to lend us a vehicle to use while ours was in the shop.

We drove the Bronco to the garage and impatiently waited as they cleaned and vacuumed out our "loaner" car. The least of my concerns was to drive a clean car. "Come on; hurry up, "I grumbled to myself. I would have liked to have seen the looks on our faces when they handed us the keys to an ancient, maroon Chrysler LeBaron with very worn velour seats. We were relieved that we were in a town where no one would recognize us. At least we had something to drive.

The next morning I had to make a trip to pick up five baby skunks and a pair of kit foxes. Off I went down the dirt road on my seventy-five mile journey in the maroon LeBaron. My first stop was for the five orphan skunks that were carefully placed in the carrier and loaded onto the red velour back seat. Thirty miles later I added the two foxes to my collection. The next thirty miles were spent saying every prayer I ever learned in my Catholic upbringing. "Oh God, please don't let them spray, PLEASE?" My prayers were answered and we were able to return the LeBaron smelling just as nice as when we picked it up.

June the third marked the onslaught of fawns that would turn our lives into a living nightmare. The first was a two day old antelope buck. PLEASE let him cooperate! Visions of Sugar bouncing off the walls like a racquetball danced in my head.

Another antelope buck came on the fourteenth of June. Two of one species is always easier to handle. The two little bucks instantly became best friends. Angelo was the older and Archie the younger. They gadded about like two large grasshoppers, their huge black eyes scanning everything that moved or didn't move for that matter. To the two of them everything was new and exciting and they didn't want to miss a thing.

They would egg each other on to get a closer look at something that they were curious about but not certain of. One would be in front of the other and the back up seemed to be saying, "Go ahead, I dare you. I'll go if you do. You're a chicken."

Just about that time the llamas, who have about the same curiosity level as the antelope, would whinny and send the two off in a flurry with their white rumps flared and their manes standing straight out like flags behind their skinny little necks. When the little fawns are getting used to their new environment it is as traumatic for me as it is for them, probably more so.

Meanwhile Sweet Potato had moved from her intensive care cage complete with heating pad to a roomier cage with a pan of water and some mud to experiment with. Although little beaver are capable of swimming soon after birth, Sweet Potato was in no hurry for swimming lessons. We began supplementing her baby food diet with natural foods such as aspen and willow bark. She was also very fond of carrots.

Her baby food was dispensed through a large plastic eyedropper as she sat in my lap. Her little front feet would grasp the dropper tightly as her large webbed back feet protruded in front of her. It didn't take her long to perfect this method and not get the gluey stuff all over her face. At least now she didn't have to complain about cleanup time.

She was quite capable of eating her cereal out of her bowl, but the two of us still enjoyed "eyedropper time". When she was hungry she would let me know by holding up her little clenched fists as if she were blowing a horn. She seemed very content in her cardboard box lodge for the time being.

In the interim between the two antelope fawns, Tom made a trip to pick up a whitetail buck fawn. The little buck had been living in a house in a straw bed behind the living room sofa. He was thrilled with his new outdoor environment and his two strange looking little friends. He was a very playful, ornery little critter and became known as Onray.

June seventeenth brought us an exceptionally large mule deer fawn. She was obviously older than the other fawn, very independent, and rather difficult to handle. We put her indoors to try to settle her down so that she would not harm herself. She wasn't thrilled with this idea and proceeded to texture the screen door on the intensive care room. Within a few hours she was willing to cooperate and readily accepted the bottle of milk that she was offered. She was then moved to the outdoor pen with Onray, Archie and Angelo.

She didn't quite understand the ear sucking ritual after bottles and would stare from a distance as the others attacked me. In a few moments she too would sneak over, grasp my ear and give me a few nibbles. It really was nice to have them so independent. She didn't have much to do with us except at feeding time. We simply called her Big Doe. Big Doe and Onray teemed up and spent most of the day out of the pen.

On June twenty-third the fawn "clown" of the year arrived. At a nearby prison with an honor system and outdoor facilities for farming, an inmate had found a new born fawn and watched to see if the mother would return. After waiting a reasonable length of time he picked her up. The inmate was somehow able to care for, feed and nurture this little creature that expressed so much love and appreciation to him. After eight days the system caught on to his activity and the fawn had to be taken away from him.

I know what these little things can give you, the feeling that they are able to bring out of you. Even as I write this my eyes fill with tears for the inmate that had to surrender possibly the only living thing that had ever loved him.

Henrietta

Tom was allowed to enter the prison grounds with the game warden to obtain the fawn and visit with the inmate. The convict had managed to get cows milk to feed the fawn and antibiotics from the prison infirmary for her bout with diarrhea. As the little doe was put in the carrier to leave, the tall, thin inmate touched her through the wire door saying his goodbye. He would never see her again. Maybe it is because of the way that we acquired "Henrietta" that she has always had a special quality about her.

Henrietta was always a bit more curious than the others. She studied things and always seemed to be thinking. Henry of course was the first to be able to leap up onto the wood deck and help me paint. She was fascinated by everything!

Another one of Henrietta's favorite activities was dancing. She could twist and spin with the best of rock stars. Out of the clear blue sky, Henry would jump straight up in the air and do a three hundred and sixty degree turn, land and then do the same movement in the opposite direction. Tom called her routines "air doe bics." You could tell by the look on her face that the moves she was putting herself through were just for fun.

By now Sweet Potato had moved to yet another larger cage in the barn. She was still not crazy about the swimming aspect of being a beaver, but was very actively involved with mud. Her large shallow pan of mud and water was carefully worked on daily. She scraped the mud into a little dam that captured the water in the lower end of her pool. Amazing! She was already practicing her natural skills as an engineer. She also scented the mud pile to mark it as her territory. On the opposite side of her cage was her newly built wood lodge. Sweet Potato spent most of the day in her lodge napping and privately grooming herself.

One morning as I came out to do the necessary chores like cage cleaning, I heard a fussing sound coming from her cage. Sweet Potato was in the doorway of her house sitting up with clenched fists and staring at something in the opposite corner.

A garden snake had the audacity to enter her space and she wanted it OUT! Shaking her little fists, she was saying in beaver language, "Get it out of here! Get it out of here NOW!" She was much happier with the nasty thing gone.

Another morning she was again very upset and fussy. While grooming she had managed to wipe the gluey baby food from her mouth and rubbed it in her eyes. The pasty stuff then dried and she was unable to open her eyes. She darted out of her lodge to let me know that she was totally blind and not very happy about it. Her eyesight and disposition were quickly restored with a warm wet cloth.

On June twenty-fifth, another fawn was brought to us after two young boys had rescued him from a shallow mine shaft. The ordeal left him with a deep cut on his right front leg. An injury of this type can be very stressful on such a delicate creature.

His diet was supplemented with special nutrients and he was placed on antibiotics. A cut this size could drain him of the much needed energy to heal. He obviously loved the extra attention that he was getting and when we were not available for his every whim, he cried and mewed like a cat. We named the puny little guy Wimpy. Wimpy began maturing before our eyes and was doing very well for his slow start. The hoofed mammal collection was now at six and was very manageable. Five days later, however, number seven entered our lives.

Fallina, as she was named by the rehabilitator that brought her to us, was an absolutely gorgeous golden whitetail doe. She was the living essence of a fairy tale. Every move that she made was done as though she had studied the finest ballerinas. She didn't run, or charge for her bottle like the others, she made an entrance. She was like an apparition as she appeared from the thickets of scrub oak: always alert, head held high with a perfect arc to her neck. Her tail fanned as she held it erect, the golden center trimmed in snow white. When Fallina was through with her bottles, she didn't just leave, she vanished. Fallina was immediately attracted to Onray, the little ornery whitetail buck.

14

THE OR-FAWN-AGE

July second, was it raining fawns or what? The typical phone call! "Would you take a baby fawn?" Ten minutes later, "We forgot to tell you. There are two." I can't even imagine saying, "Oh sure I'll take one, but two, forget it." So much for the empty nest syndrome!

I picked up Arty and Gwenadeer at the wildlife office. Both tiny fawns were calmly tucked side by side inside a pet carrier, trusting anyone who happened to come their way. We now had nine hungry fawns with only four hands and two sets of knees with which to hold bottles. This necessitated plans for an easier way to feed them.

Tom, the problem solver, designed the MFF600, as we jokingly called it. MFF stood for Multi-Fawn Feeder, 600 because it could handle six punching, shoving, nursing fawns with no problem. The MFF was an ingenious idea. It was a three foot by five inch piece of plywood with six holes into which bottle necks were placed and then tops and nipples screwed on to hold the bottles in place. It was cheap and very efficient. Tom could now hold the feeder and take care of six fawns while I still hand fed the stragglers.

MFF

The total count at this time was two antelope, two whitetail, and five mule deer. We also had two opossums, two kit foxes, one beaver, and five raccoons. The fawns, however, took up most of our time. Where was Jessica when I really needed her help?

A perky little mule doe was next to arrive. She was found in the forest with no mother. Most of the fawns that we get should never have been picked up by well intentioned humans. Mothers leave their fawns after feeding them and visit only two or three times a day to nurse. The fawns are licked by the mother and kept scentless to protect them from predators. The fawn does not start to follow its mother until it is about one month old. Mom is close by but frightened by humans who happen to stumble upon the tiny spotted creatures hiding in the grass. When she returns, her baby is gone. I don't even like to think about how the doe must feel to find that her fawn has disappeared.

Barbie Doe, our newest fawn, was the victim of this unfortunate situation. The only way to describe Barbie is "cute". The perky little doe had been learning the fine art of sleeping in a water bed with the couple who "rescued" her. Suddenly it dawned on them that they didn't have the necessary room to raise a deer fawn.

Barbie was confused with her new surroundings. "What! No waterbed? Only straw in that wood shelter to lie on?" At the orfawnage, Barbie had what she really needed: the out of doors and real deer friends.

She was instantly attracted to Big Doe, probably assuming that she was her mother because of her size. It took her several days to associate us with feeding. She spent a few hungry days hiding so well that we couldn't find her or get her to come out. Big Doe was good for Barbie. She was very independent and Barbie wanted to be with her instead of us which was the best possible thing to have happen.

By this time it was getting pretty difficult to tell them apart. Each, however, had different facial markings. If we saw them from the rear, forget it, except for the whitetails and the antelope, who were obviously marked differently.

Barbie had a very unique face. Her large almond eyes accented her little pug nose. Even today, although I seldom see her as a yearling, I can pick her out because of her face. She was most definitely a "Barbie Doe".

Our days were now very scheduled. The very first thing that happened at 5:30 A.M. was fawn feeding. There was no other choice. They were always ready to eat and when they saw or heard us, they had to have bottles of warm milk, lots of bottles of warm milk. After the morning feeding we left the gate open on their pen and let them out to explore the yard and find places to hide until the noon meal.

Sweet Potato was fed after the fawns had dispersed and settled down. Although she could very easily eat by herself, the two of us still enjoyed eyedropper time at least twice a day.

One day out of the clear blue sky, the Potato was ready to swim. Her large yellow swimming pool was filled and ready for her. I carried her over to the pool and held her at the edge. To my amazement she slid gently out of my hands and into the water. Then she just floated there like a cork for several minutes feeling the cool water all around her plump little body. Baby beavers are very buoyant and it would take time for her fur to get conditioned so that she could dive.

Now that Sweet Potato was ready to swim, we built her a large cage with her pool filling one whole end. On the opposite side of the cage was her lodge. Now when she had the urge to swim, she simply had to exit her lodge, waddle a few feet to the edge of the pool and launch herself. Because beaver defecate in the water, her pool was scrubbed and filled with fresh water twice a day.

15

MORPHANS

The day after Barbie arrived, a little mule doe had walked up to some fishermen on the river. Assuming that she had been abandoned by her mother, the men picked her up and called the game warden. The little doe was very weak and not able to stand when the game warden brought her to us. Because of her condition, the fishermen had been right to believe that the little fawn had lost its mother.

She was given the usual check up for new fawns and fed with a stomach tube because she was too weak to nurse. After being hydrated she was left to rest in the intensive care room. When I checked on her in about an hour she seemed much stronger and was now able to stand, but the battle had just begun.

Four hours later she still would not nurse. She wouldn't suck anything, bottle, ears, cloths, nothing. She needed nourishment so we tube fed her again. It sometimes takes a few feedings before they get used to the idea of taking their milk from a bottle.

This continued for several days. We could not get her to take a bottle. The little fawn seemed so confused. She would attempt to nurse and after an ounce or two she would stop and tilt her head as though she had forgotten what she was trying to do. We called the little doe "Doepy" because of her constant state of confusion.

I tried not to get too attached to Doepy. I knew something was wrong. She seemed so confused, even the look in her eyes was not normal. However, Doepy was alive and would be given every opportunity to stay that way.

Two days later Felipe joined us, "Strange Felipe", another perfect whitetail. Whitetails just seem to have a certain air about them. He was found floating down an irrigation ditch by a farmer who reluctantly surrendered him to the

Division of Wildlife. I really can't blame people for wanting to keep them. They are such splendid little creations.

Felipe brought the count to twelve fawns; three whitetail, two antelope, and seven mule deer. The MFF 600 was no longer sufficient and the MFF 800 went into production.

Felipe was put in the intensive care room. Maybe he would be good for Doepy. He was very young and being indoors for a few days wouldn't hurt him. He eagerly downed his milk, briefly inspected Doepy, and slipped off to hide behind the bale of straw in the corner. He knew exactly what he was and what he had to do. Doepy just cocked her head and seemed to ponder whether what just happened really did happen.

Outside frolicked ten little fawns who would soon have the company of Felipe, and then there was dear little Doepy. What was going to happen with her?

To get the fawns to return to the pen at night we scheduled feeding time early enough to round them all up and get them inside the pen and close the gate before we fed them. One evening after the roundup and feeding frenzy, I realized that Henrietta hadn't come for her bottles. After searching for her I found her lying in the shelter. Her tummy was bloated to twice its normal size. As I lifted her I expected her to pop. I began massaging her and trying to relieve some of the gas that had built up inside her.

Since it was getting dark outside I decided to take her indoors and work with her. Our vet suggested using Gas-X and as we administered it through a syringe, Felipe and Doepy watched in amazement. I decided to stay with the threesome that night so that I could keep a close eye on Henry. She seemed fairly comfortable. Again I bedded down on the straw covered cement floor and tried to get some rest.

The Gas-X was working; about ten o'clock Henry was obviously feeling better and getting thinner. She got up and came over to pester me. I tried to ignore her by covering my head with a blanket but she proceeded to get to my hair and ears even through the barricade.

She was feeling much better and getting on my nerves. Suddenly Doepy made a connection somewhere in her feeble little mind, jumped up and joined Henry in chewing on me. I came to the conclusion that it was time for Henry to go back outside. If I wanted to be alive in the morning I had no other choice.

Since she hadn't had her evening feed I decided to get her some milk and then put her out, or should I say THROW her out. When I returned to the room with the bottles, I was attacked not only by Henry but also by dear little Doepy. This was the first time that she took a full bottle without getting confused. From that day on Doepy no longer had to be fed with a tube. I guess I have Henry and her gassy stomach to thank.

Since Doepy could now compete for her bottles with the best of them, she and Felipe graduated to the outdoor pen. We now had twelve assorted fawns living around our house. Going outdoors was very risky. If they heard us or saw us, they immediately assumed that it was feeding time.

The MFF 800 was now in use. With Tom holding it and me holding the MFF 600 we could feed all twelve fawns simultaneously. We had to brace ourselves against the fence or the house to be able to hold onto the bottles while they were nursing.

I lived from feeding to feeding. We could almost catch our breath after the evening meal because after they ate they were ready to bed down until morning. Twelve fawns were a bit crowded in the pen so we began leaving the pen open at night. The older and braver ones could now choose to bed down wherever they wanted.

When morning came and we mustered up enough courage to go out with the bottle racks, the fawns came from all directions. They ran out of the bushes, out of the pen, out of the shelter, out from under the deck. I really expected them to start falling out of the sky. With this many we would surely have to wean them earlier. HA!

Doepy kept the closest vigil on the house. We were not going to out smart her. The frail little doe would appear out of thin air or simply bed down on the wood deck facing the door. We would sneak Doepy extra bottles during the day because of her weakened condition.

Archie and Angelo were the worst. They seemed to know exactly when we tip-toed out the door trying to avoid them. They would slink out of nowhere smacking their black lips with their licorice tongues. Their huge black eyes never seemed to blink. They were strange, but they were very cooperative for antelope so I couldn't complain. We finally started giving them bottles of warm water just to get rid of them.

On the twentieth of July a game warden whom we had never met before called and politely said that he had heard that we cared for orphaned wildlife. I proudly told him, "Yes, we sure did, what could we help him with?"

A family had picked up a (you guessed it) fawn and were raising it in their house. "Did we think that it would be possible to put it back into the wild?" I assured him that I believed it was very possible and we made arrangements to meet him at eight o'clock that evening to pick up the fawn.

What should have been a one hour trip turned into a six hour one because of a severe thunderstorm that delayed the officer. Tom arrived home about one o'clock with John Deer. The delay didn't seem to bother big burly John and he quickly downed several bottles and some apples and bedded down in the inside room.

In the morning John was brought outdoors and introduced to his huge new family. John liked them all but he liked people a lot better and wanted to follow Tom or me around all day. This continued for several days so we tried very hard to ignore him. It didn't take him very long and soon he was spending his time with his "deer" friends.

Sweet Potato by now was growing into a gorgeous young beaver. Her oiled fur stayed dry now as she dove in her larger pool in the driveway. She was only allowed in the large pool while Tom or I were out in the yard to supervise. In the morning as I cleaned her cage and pool, Sweet Potato entertained the deer who came to the edge of her pool to watch.

Henrietta, of course, was drawn to this scene like a magnet. There were several occasions when Henry climbed right into the pool with her. Sweet Potato thought it was great fun to dive in and out Henry's legs and then surface nose to nose with her. When Henry finished playing with her in the pool she would then come over and climb into the cage with me to supervise the cleanup.

Sweet little Doepy was a big fan of Sweet Potatoes. Doepy loved to watch the strange thing disappear under the water and then come up somewhere else.

When Sweet Potato was tired of swimming, she would climb out of her pool and waddle the fifteen feet or so to her cage and climb in.

She was now stripping the bark from aspen and willow and then piling the stripped branches in the doorway of her lodge. She also pulled leaves and twigs inside for bedding. Occasionally she would have a house cleaning day all by herself. She was wonderful to watch. Everything inside her lodge was pushed to the doorway and added to the debris in the entrance way. At night she would carry new leaves and bedding to her clean lodge.

16

NIGHTMARE

All thirteen fawns were thriving. Even our frail little Doepy was doing much better than we had anticipated. The bakers dozen managed to drink about forty baby bottles a day. The pen was open all the time now and some of the older fawns like Archie, Angelo, Fallina, Onray, and the Big Doe were venturing farther from home.

It is always very stressful when they start to go farther. My vet told me once that I worried about them too much. He laughed and seemed to understand my feelings when I replied, "How would you like to have thirteen of your kids out learning to drive the car, all at once?"

Within the next two weeks Sweet Potato would be leaving to join a colony of beaver that had already begun work in their new location. Things were very hectic but going very well.

The peace was destroyed during the last week of July. On the morning of July twenty-eighth, Angelo, our oldest antelope did not come for his bottle. I was mildly concerned, but convinced that he would show up before long, starving to death and licking his lips.

He still hadn't come home by the midday feeding. I spent the rest of the day searching for him or for some sign of him. He was nowhere to be found. Something had happened to him. At this young age they do not leave home so suddenly.

We felt helpless. Perhaps he had followed some wild deer. They were so curious. I was convinced that he would be home by night fall. Twelve fawns came to eat. Angelo was not one of them. We never saw Angelo again. We searched everywhere. There was no sign of a struggle with dogs or coyotes. No trace of blood or hair. What could possibly have happened to him?

Angelo's lifetime buddy, Archie, was as concerned as we were. Only somehow I think he already knew. How I wished that he could have told me. That night Archie danced around in the driveway, bucking and kicking and trying to explain something. The next morning neither he nor Fallina, the whitetail princess, showed up to eat. They too, had vanished during the night.

I called Steve, our good friend and Division of Wildlife officer and told him what was happening to the fawns. My fear deepened when he told me that it was very likely that a mountain lion was preying on our little herd.

This seemed the most logical explanation for their disappearance. To a mountain lion, a fawn this size was very easy prey. They were then carried off, which would explain why we hadn't found any trace of them. In our search efforts Tom did find lion tracks in the mud about a half mile from our house. Tracks of any kind were not visible close to home because of the thick wild grass cover.

The next few weeks were terrifying. I could function as long as it was daylight, but as nighttime came I began to fill with terror. We took turns staying up during the night. During this time we would spotlight the area frequently or drive around slowly making noise. We would make such a commotion that the thing would never come back.

Fortunately the area in which we live is not heavily populated so we were not interfering with neighbors. The ones that did live close by knew what was going on and appreciated it because they had domestic animals of their own. I knew the bottom had to fall out. Things had been going too smoothly.

We have an open deck off the loft of our three story house. This was a great place to sleep and a terrific lookout point. From the deck we could spotlight the entire area and pick up the glow of predator eyes. Predator eyes give off a yellow glow. The reflection of deer eyes is green.

I tried to realize that what was going on was the most natural way of life for them. Fifty to seventy percent of wild fawns are taken by predators or killed in accidents. This thought, however, did not make it any easier to cope with. They were disappearing and there was absolutely nothing that we could do about it. Lion experts also forecasted nothing but doom when they told me that the lion would continue to feed on the fawns because they were such easy prey.

By August things usually slow down and we are able to relax and enjoy everyone growing up before we have to return to our jobs. Although totally stressed out, we still managed to give everyone else the best possible living conditions.

Two days after Archie and Fallina vanished we took Sweet Potato to her new home. I laughed as I held her in my lap while we drove. The night before the sheriff had driven into the yard about ten o'clock to see how things were going with the mountain lion problem. Nosy Sweet Potato, to get a better view, climbed up the wire on her cage to stand on the edge of her pool. She stretched up as far as she could, holding the wire with her little front feet. She was quite agitated and demanded to know what the sheriff was doing in her yard. As she stretched higher and higher she lost her grip and toppled over backward into her pool.

Sweet Potato & Fawns

The Potato's new home would be on a large ranch about forty miles from us. The owner wished to have some beaver ponds and five relocated beaver were working on the project. One large pond and a lodge had already been constructed.

I carried her over to the edge and set her down a couple of feet from the shore. She quickly waddled into the water and gently slid in, just as she did the first time that she decided to swim in her yellow plastic pool.

I could feel her excitement as she dove several feet and surfaced with a very contented look. Over and over she dove and explored every nook and cranny of the pond. She no longer had the confines of a plastic bottom. Now she could go deeper and stay down much longer.

I always wished that we could have given her more swimming room, but watching her now only proved that she learned what she really needed to know in those bright colored swimming pools. What joy she must have been feeling. We watched for quite some time and only once did she come out of the water. We had been standing back a distance from the shore just enjoying watching her discover her new found freedom.

To say goodbye, I walked to the edge of the pond. She swam over to the shore and in her clumsy land walk lumbered up to my feet and stood up as though she wanted to shake my hand. I scooped her up for the last time and we said our goodbyes. A very special bond was severed as she glided back into the water. A few feet from shore she slapped the water with her tail and swam to the farthest part of the pond, never looking back.

We turned and walked back to the car. It had been a very special time. Sweet Potato made me forget the nightmare that we must return to at home.

The remaining ten fawns accepted things as they were. I wished that I could. The setting of the sun evoked a feeling deep inside that was destroying me. I just wanted night to be over. Why couldn't it be daylight for twenty four hours?

On the way home from taking Sweet Potato, I mentioned to Tom that Doepy needed some extra attention. I still worried about her. That morning as we had readied Sweet Potato for her journey, Doepy watched us pack up her friend to leave.

That same afternoon we were hit by a terrible thunder and lightening storm. All of the fawns headed for the shelter of the oak brush except Doepy. I couldn't stand to see the little doe standing out in the severe weather. I ran out and brought her into the house until the storm was over. We towel dried her, fixed her some warm milk and waited out the storm.

A friend called and as I visited with her, Doepy putsied around the table nibbling on the phone cord and my clothes and then left to visit with Tom in the living room. Several minutes later I went to see what they were doing. Tears filled my eyes as I entered the room and found my six foot tall husband sound asleep on the floor. Curled up between his shoulder and neck was little Doepy, she too was fast asleep. I left them alone until the storm passed and then returned Doepy to the outdoors to enjoy the late afternoon sun with her friends.

The following day, at the evening feeding, all the fawns arrived at the front door except Doepy. After the pushing and shoving and feeding were over I went to look for her. I found her just around the corner of the house lying with her neck and head turned back. I quickly scooped up her nearly weightless little body and carried her inside. I knew that there was nothing that I could possibly do but cradle her and sooth her as her life slipped away.

Doepy was a very special little doe. Right from the start I knew that she would not be with us for long. I can still see her popping up in the least expected places ready for just a little extra attention. It is comforting to know that her short life was a very happy time, both for her and us.

17

VIDAL AND SASSOON

Two days after Doepy left us we became the proud parents of two infant raccoons. The day was cold and miserable and they were coming to us from a town about eighty miles away. The two tiny orphans had been tossed in a large cardboard box with a filthy old rag by a farmer. He had killed their mother with a board when she startled him as he entered his barn.

The two sightless babies (their eyes do not open until they are about three weeks old) were covered with their own feces and were cold to the touch. My friend Lee quickly scooped up the smelly little critters and tucked them inside her shirt, close to her body to warm them up.

We drove home with the heater in the car set as high as it would go. When we got them home we cleaned them up. We laughed as we shampooed and blow dried them and they became known as Vidal and Sassoon.

Vidal, the little girl, was much stronger than her little brother Sassoon. After they were cleaned and fed they were put in an intensive care cage. They had soft flannel baby blankets for a nest. It was lined with a heating pad. Above them we placed a blue twenty-five watt light bulb for added warmth. Chilling is probably the worst thing that could possibly happen to them, but they were now toasty warm and comfortable.

Vidal

Vidal ate vigorously every four hours but little Sassoon struggled to down his half ounce of milk. The two snuggled with each other for companionship and when he died three days later my heart broke as I watched the tiny little creature search for her brother. She needed something to replace him. I keep plenty of stuffed toy animals just for this reason.

Vidal was given a large stuffed dog that sat up like a mother raccoon when she nurses her young. Vidal found the soft fur of the toy to be very comforting and spent her sleeping time snuggled in the lap of her surrogate mother. Ticking away behind the stuffed toy was an alarm clock that gave her added security.

The loss of the little raccoon didn't make it any easier to deal with my fear of night time. We were exhausted from our night watch. We had to face it! We couldn't stay awake forever. It had been eleven days since the disappearance of the two antelope and the whitetail doe. Maybe, just maybe, we were successful at scaring the lion away.

On August eighth, the day that Sassoon died, I made a stupid mistake. I let our three silver foxes out of their cage assuming that they would return in the evening for their meal. I guess I just needed to release something and since it couldn't be me, Why not the foxes?

Out they came, eager to explore the world that they had seen only through the wire cage. Some days should not happen, this was one of them! The foxes proceeded to torment everything, especially the fawns. All day long I tried to catch them. They would come close but wouldn't let me touch them.

The largest of the three was a male. He was in the deer pen with no way to get out but the gate. I positioned myself and tried to act nonchalant. As he headed toward me I pounced on him. I was lying in the dirt, my right hand holding him by the scruff of the neck, his mouth latched onto my forearm. I realized that he was winning.

I had no choice but to let him go. I couldn't stand the pain any longer. I let go. He ran off to torment something else and I went in to clean my wounds. By evening, I knew that they had no intention of turning themselves in without a fight.

Meanwhile a group from the nature center had brought up two little rock squirrels for us to finish raising and release. "Please go home," I thought to myself as they hesitated to leave. It was getting dark and I had no intention of leaving these three monsters out all night long. Tom would catch them when he got home. I could always count on him.

At nightfall they began moving to the barn. We finally managed to corner them and catch them with noose poles and heavy gloves. They were as tired as we were. They would have to remain caged until they could be released somewhere else. Their time would come and you could bet that it would not be anywhere near my yard.

My arm throbbed as I dragged myself into bed that night. We both needed sleep and sleep came quickly. It was the first night that we spent in a real bed in more than two weeks. The windows and screen door were wide open. Neither of us had the strength to climb the extra set of stairs to our surveillance center.

About two o'clock I was awakened out of a deep sleep by something that sounded like the meow of a cat. I made it to the top of the fourteen step flight of stairs in two leaps and was out on the upper deck spotlighting in less than thirty seconds. As I scanned the area with the light, Tom was already dressed and outside.

There were numerous fawns scattered around as usual, not seeming to be alarmed. There were several large deer across the road watching something up the hill from us. The llamas were all in the corner of their pen staring in the same direction as the deer. In the driveway was a large stray tom cat. Could that have been what woke me up? I hoped that was all it was.

I joined Tom outside and several of the fawns had already gathered around him and were acting as they usually do (hungry). Not all were accounted for but things didn't seem that unusual. Hoping that all we had heard was a house cat fight, we returned to bed.

In the morning, however, as bottles were dispensed, three of the fawns did not show up. In a few moments Barbie came and in a few more John arrived, both seeming slightly upset. Wimpy was not among the group. Wimpy our little mine shaft fawn was evidently the latest victim. We never saw him or any sign of him again. The terror deepened.

We assumed that whatever was taking the fawns was coming down from the mountain because of the direction that the llamas and deer had been looking. We widened our search but found nothing. We were not eating well and the intermittent sleep that we were getting was not enough to keep up with the strain. When was this going to stop? I didn't think that I could take another lost fawn.

At a time like this all the experts offer their advice. I was told to lock them up at night. What purpose would that serve? If a lion did get in the pen, the fawns would kill themselves trying to flee with no place to go except into a chain link fence. If they were out, they at least had a chance to escape.

We were down to nine fawns. Four had vanished into thin air. Things just seemed to deteriorate. While Felipe, our youngest whitetail buck, was trying to nurse I noticed blood on the top of his head. He didn't take his usual three to four bottles and after the feeding frenzy, I went to get a closer look at him.

Another blow! Felipe had a broken jaw. He was probably hit by one of the large does as he pestered her. His jaw protruded as though he was chewing a huge wad of bubble gum. Felipe could not nurse with his crooked jaw. He was only about six weeks old and had to nurse at least another two to three months.

I solved his nursing problem simply by holding my index finger under his jaw, lining it up with the top jaw as he nursed. With the jaw bones lined up he was able to suck. It worked beautifully and within six weeks his jaw had healed perfectly. At last something went right!

The school year was quickly approaching and the next three weeks passed without anymore nighttime disappearances. The night before our first day of work we climbed into bed with lots of mixed feelings. It isn't easy to go back even after a relaxing summer. Ours had been far from relaxing.

The fawns would be missing their mid-day feeding. Tom had a wonderful idea. He took a collapsible water jug and replaced the cap with a bottle nipple. It worked like a charm. I even tested it myself by getting down on hands and knees and took the nipple in my mouth. The downward push sent the water through the nipple and the fawns were able to satisfy their nursing needs without us around.

The night was again disrupted. At two-thirty we awoke to the sounds of bleating fawns, a sound that they make when trapped or injured. It is a terrible cry. The beam of my spotlight caught eight pairs of eyes running toward the yard from the pasture across the road. One fawn was headed up the road. They were probably frightened by the coyotes who occasionally roam there. Convinced that they were all accounted for we returned to bed.

When I awoke at four-thirty I was pleased to see all nine fawns dancing on the deck eager to have breakfast. I went in to warm bottles and then went out the front door to feed them. In the dim porch light all seemed to be okay except John who was not able to take his bottle. I examined him closely and saw that he had been bitten on the face. He had puncture wounds around his mouth, nose and eyes. I cleaned his wounds and he went to lie down by a tree in the front yard.

I had to go to work wondering if he would be alive when we got home. Deer are so susceptible to stress. The injuries themselves were not severe and the best thing for him was rest and quiet. To make things even worse my eyes and face were covered in a terrible red rash because of my reaction to raccoon hair. The salt from my tears was not exactly soothing.

John had evidently had an encounter with a coyote. Could that have been what happened to our other four fawns? Were they too small to escape? Or was it a mountain lion? We never knew what happened. If John did live he would have learned a valuable lesson that he would never forget.

I was not very eager to go to work. The morning consisted of a teacher's meeting at a local high school. I looked terrific. A face that looked like a raspberry patch, eyes half swollen shut and hair that looked as though it had been styled with a rake. The clothes that I was wearing had been ripped off the hangars at the last minute.

Of course everyone had to ask how my summer was and how all the animals were. This sent the tears flowing again and made the rash even worse. All that I could think of was going home to see if John was still by the tree and alive. The day was long and we drove home in silence. We arrived at home shortly after four o'clock and John was still by the tree, hurting, but hungry. A feeling of relief flowed through me as he nursed. My spirits lifted as I did my various chores.

18

THE SEASON COMES TO AN END

◆

(OR DOES IT?)

It didn't take long to get back into the swing of working. We had plenty of time before we left for work in the morning to enjoy feeding time and then watch the fawns leave for the day. Fortunately we have jobs that allow us to arrive home early enough to have nice long evenings. I finally got to a skin doctor and my face returned to normal. Vidal was thriving and enjoyed coming out in the evening to entertain and play with the deer.

September tenth brought Vidal a friend. After downing a large tree, a woodcutter found a little orphan coon and brought her to us. Vidal now had a sister and we both felt better about her situation. Now she had someone to do real coon things with. Again we had Vidal and Sassoon.

Most of our fawns were approaching four months of age and the thought occurred to me that I should wean them soon. I began watering down their morning and evening meals but they still loved it. Oh well!

Three weeks into the school year we finally began to relax. On the twentieth of September we were pitched backward three months. An archery hunter had found a newborn fawn and of course "rescued it". When the call came, I hesitated to believe that it could be as young as they said it was. The fawn was relayed to us and sure enough, there he was, chocolate brown hair dotted with hundreds of milky white spots. That meant real milk feedings again, at least twice a day.

The little buck was incredibly handsome and we named him Don Fawn. Donnie had spent the day in the wildlife office about forty-five miles away. Several attempts during the day had only managed to get about two ounces of milk into the little guy. When the little buck saw Tom, it was as though he recognized him as a savior of deer and lunged into his arms and began sucking on him. He was starving. He seemed to realize that he was going to a terrific place. Donnie and Tom always had a very special relationship.

He had no problem taking the milk that was offered him at the orfawnage. He then met all of his new friends and found a comfortable place up against the house and dozed until sunset. It was as though he had been there all of his short little life. At nightfall I put Donnie in the intensive care room so that I could give him a feeding during the night.

One night in the room was okay, but he wanted to be outdoors with his new family. I fed him again in the morning and then left him outside with the others. He was about a third their size but they readily accepted him. After all he was a deer and an orphan deer at that.

At 4:00 P.M. when we drove into the yard the parade up the sidewalk to meet us was led by the tiny buck. He had the routine all figured out and it made it a lot easier on us. We were still bottle feeding twice a day. The morning feeding was shortly after five o'clock. It was worth our lifes to walk out on the front porch with the container of bottles. One morning as I stepped outside into the gathered crowd, the nine fawns tripped me and down I went, disappearing into the center of thirty-six little pointed hooves. Tom managed to get me back on my feet and retrieve the scattered bottles before they trampled me to death.

Hunting season was approaching rapidly. I had my magic marker ready to X off the days until it ended. Opening day of the season brought heavy snow and very cold temperatures. This cheered me up. At least if someone had to hunt they could be cold and miserable.

Donnie had since found the shelter of our large open front barn. He had several large straw beds, water, hay and shelter from the snow and the cold. The little guy was still in spots and did not have a sufficient winter coat.

That night as I sat with Donnie in the barn, I witnessed a Norman Rockwell painting come to life. Tom dressed in jeans, a black and gray buffalo plaid jacket, and black baseball cap walked up our two hundred yard long driveway to place a

"NO HUNTING" sign on the fence across the road. It was dark outside except for the light from the misty red sky and snow covered ground. As he walked, the other eight fawns gathered around his heels and followed him to the fence. They hovered around him as he wired the sign to the fence. The only color visible in the scene was the fluorescent red letters on the sign. It was an incredible sight and even now I can close my eyes and see the whole picture as if were happening at this very moment.

We made it through the hunting season without incident until the last day. Tom was going to ride with Steve, the game warden. They left about 6:00 A.M. and as they drove off laughingly told me to stay out of trouble. Who me?

The sun had not come up yet and all the fawns and Vidal and Sassoon were with me in the yard. We decided to go for a walk to celebrate the end of the season. The twelve of us headed up the road to the sunny hillside to warm up; as we approached the top of the hill I heard voices and then saw four or five deer running straight toward us. I knew the voices had to be those of hunters so I shouted to let them know that I was in their line of fire. They must have heard me and no shots were fired.

I knew that no one was supposed to be in the area and was irritated that someone was trespassing. We reached our hilltop destination and from where I stood I saw three hunters clad in their orange hunting gear. They were at least a quarter of a mile away and froze when they heard me yell, "Get out of here, you are on private property." I yelled so loudly that eight of the fawns that had come with me exploded in eight different directions and disappeared. That left me, Donnie, Vidal and Sassoon on the hilltop. The hunters heard me, turned around and left. I had no idea who they were, just that they had no business in the area.

The four of us returned home to try to get through the rest of the day. Steve and Tom were still out patrolling when I got a phone call from a friend in our small town. He and his friend were out hunting and came across an adult doe standing motionless in a field. They approached her and she made no attempt to run. She had not been shot and they didn't want to just leave her so they picked her up and brought the dazed doe to our yard in the back of a jeep. I really didn't know what to do. I decided to tranquilize her and put her in the shade to rest and we could decide what to do later in the day.

I went into the house to get a shot to give her, leaving the two orange clad hunters sitting with the doe in the back of the jeep. They felt bad about her and sat with chin in hands just looking at her.

About this time Tom and Steve drove into the yard. They saw the hunters, the jeep and the deer. They didn't see me. Steve said to Tom, "What did she do, chain them to the jeep until we got here?" The two were very relieved when they found out that I was not holding the hunters hostage and did not in any way harm them. They were simply concerned and caring hunters.

We carried the tranquilized doe into the shade and laid her down. Donnie came out to see what was going on and saw the large deer sleeping under the tree. He walked over to her, nuzzled and licked her and then tucked himself in next to her warm body for the rest of the afternoon.

Our two friends Lee and Casey were coming up that evening to celebrate the seasons end. We fixed a terrific meal and toasted with an expensive bottle of wine. Just as we finished eating and were sitting around the table feeling nice and relaxed the telephone rang. It was Steve. The hunters whom I yelled at had called and turned me in for hunter harassment. If that were the case, I wished that I had given them a worse time.

They had a lot of nerve. They were trespassing. They had no permission from the owner to be on the land and they turned me in for harassment! Steve just laughed it off and told the hunters that I really was in the right to do what I had done. I did have permission from the land owner to keep hunters off his land. These hunters happened to be the same ones who, on the last day of the previous season, shot a beautiful buck at the corner of our property, right in front of me.

Well it was over for a least another year. I had purposely been trying to avoid any sightings of large bucks. I knew that Tim and Tim would be likely candidates for this season. I really did not want to know. As I said before, hunting is part of the game.

The large mule deer was coming out of her tranquilized state and was not any better. She could not stand and did not respond to any type of stimulation. We assumed that she had been car hit and was suffering brain and spinal damage. The outlook was not good and for her own peace of mind we euthanized her the same night.

19

THE HOLIDAYS

Vidal and Sassoon were young adults now. The two were allowed their freedom in the barn and the yard during the day but were still shut in their cage at night-fall. One night I was busy and allowed the two to be out much later than usual. When I went out to put them up for the night, I heard strange noises coming from the scrub oak around the deer pen. Little Sassoon was balanced in the top of an oak, scared to death. I located Vidal in the large juniper tree, she too was terri-fied.

I helped her out of the tree and set her down. The two got right on my heels and followed me to the barn. In the glow of the yard light I noticed that Vidal was bleeding from her ear. On closer inspection I noticed that her ear had been split nearly in two and she had puncture wounds around her rump. She was very upset and did not think too much of being probed and touched.

For the next several days Vidal was not in a very good mood. She was obviously very sore and I did not try to handle her at all. She knew what she needed. We did, however, sneak antibiotics into her food.

In just a matter of days Vidal was feeling better and the abscesses from her punc-ture wounds were draining. The two liked to go for walks with us and I couldn't help but notice that Vidal's tail seemed to be dragging on the ground more than Sassoon's did. She was still sore and it would be foolish to try to handle her to get a better look.

At dawn on Thanksgiving Day a large five point buck came across the road and into our yard. It was Big Tim. The scar on his back leg that was made by a lion when he was just a yearling enabled us to identify him. I hadn't seen any of the large bucks throughout the hunting season. He had been wise enough to make it through to the next breeding season. The sight of him was enough to be thankful for this Thanksgiving.

Although the past year had been a very stressful one, we all seemed to make it through all right. We had so many things to be thankful for. We still had nine beautiful fawns that were thriving, five healthy llamas, two of whom were going to give us babies soon, Vidal and Sasson and Virgil and Virginia, the quiet opossums that would be released in the spring.

Our friends Casey and Lee and our mothers joined us in a wonderful Thanksgiving dinner. In the late afternoon the fawns came to visit and Vidal and Sassoon made an appearance. Vidal and Sassoon had been living in the barn in a large wooden goose planter. Sassoon had always been the shier of the two, but Vidal came down to see everyone. As I reached up to grab her I noticed that her tail was almost ready to fall off. It was attached by a single strand of skin. Later that evening her tail came off leaving her with a three inch bobtail. Whatever she had tangled with in the scrub oak six weeks earlier had bitten her so badly that it severed the bones of her tail.

Having no tail did not seem to bother Vidal at all. It bothered me more than it did her and it took some time before I got used to seeing a bobtail coon. At least she would be easy to identify in the future.

Each year we usually have many raccoons which make it impractical to release them from our yard. I don't think the neighborhood would appreciate it. Occasionally we have just one or two and we will let them use our yard as a halfway house. We have been very successful with the few that we have released in this manner. Vidal and Sassoon would not be relocated. They could make that choice on their own.

Again Christmas was approaching. Last year the holidays were shared with Jessica and her happy little family. Our two week Christmas vacation started out with snow and record breaking cold temperatures. It was all we could do to keep the fire going and keep the animals as comfortable as we could. We went for several days with a high temperature of only ten to fifteen degrees below zero.

Having no garage meant taking the batteries out of our vehicles so they would start the next day. I carried five gallon buckets of hot water from our second floor bathroom through the yard to the llamas and deer. During the cold spell Vidal and Sassoon completely vanished.

We worried about Donnie, our late born fawn, who was still wearing spots on his coat. He had no fat stored on his thin little body. He found shelter in the barn in the large piles of straw that I put out for him. If his coat got wet from the snow, we brought him inside to towel dry him and give him extra bottles of warm milk.

Finally the day before Christmas the cold spell broke and the twenty degree temperature felt like a heat wave. Everyone came out to bask in the warm sun. Even Vidal and Sassoon came out. They had been under a large wooden box inside the barn.

Christmas day has always been a day that Tom and I have chosen to spend alone. Other commitments are taken care of sometime during the two week holiday. Christmas day is ours. Christmas morning brought mild temperatures and a cloudless sky. About mid morning all the llamas were haltered and we left for our Christmas walk. About half a mile from our house there are two ridges, between the ridges is a valley that is sheltered from the wind and all the deer spend the coldest months of the year in the valley. As we walked the llamas, we savored the warmth and the stillness.

I saw movement to my right and in the tall pines and juniper trees appeared six of this year's fawns. They watched us to make sure that they knew us and then one by one approached us and followed us home. To me this is the magic of Christmas. They do not expect expensive gifts or elaborate meals. They share what they have, love. They truly show their appreciation for what we have done for them. They give more than they take.

Since I saw Big Tim at Thanksgiving, he had become a nightly visitor to our yard along with many others who visit us regularly during the winter months. Christmas night found him eating grain and apples in front of the window with the tree lights reflecting on him. He was now a five point buck. We had been graced with his presence for almost four years. He was now the largest buck in the herd and had everyone's respect.

We would watch him come through the llama pasture every evening. As he proudly walked toward our yard we could see deer coming from every direction to follow him. As he approached the fence to jump into our yard, all nine of our fawns would admire his great beauty and dignity.

He would graciously let the fawns eat with him but would chase the wild herd away until he was finished. I am positive that he understands what Tom and I are doing with the orphans and he is willing to help. Surely he remembers being raised here. Seeing him gives us great confidence that what we are trying to do really does work. They really can become wild.

One night I watched Big Tim rubbing his antlers on an aspen tree. Onray, the older whitetail, soaked up every movement that he made and when Tim left, Onray worked over the aspen tree with his mighty two inch antlers.

Just a few days after Christmas, a neighbor became concerned about coyotes eating on a deer carcass very close to his house. The deer had apparently been taken down by the coyotes during the severe cold weather. Food was scarce and they were coming closer to humans.

Our neighbor was very concerned and he and Tom decided that the best thing to do would be to shoot the coyote if it again came so close to the yard. I knew Tom would have a very difficult time with this because he is very fond of coyotes. On the other hand, we had nine fawns in the area and were still very concerned about their safety. I sincerely hoped that Tom would not have to deal with the situation because of his feelings. If need be though, I was sure that the safety of the fawns would dominate his feelings.

On a walk one morning with Donnie and the llamas we went behind the ridges. Tom left me and the llamas as he went over the ridge to look down at the neighbor's yard where the coyote had been staying. Sure enough there he was. He would have to do what he dreaded most. He would have to shoot a living creature that he loved.

He drew his pistol and carefully aimed at his target. Suddenly he felt something touch his leg. As he looked down he saw Donnie, the knee high little buck, tucked up next to him as if he were saying "There he is! Shoot him! Shoot him!" Tom took one look at the little mule deer's ears and thought "I have ear plugs, what is the sound of this gun going to do to those?" and put the pistol back in the holster. He didn't know that Donnie had followed him over to his lookout point as the llamas and I stayed back.

Later that day the neighbor killed the coyote. I'm sure that to this day Tom is extremely thankful that our Donnie followed him. It kept him from doing something that he truly hated to do.

On a moonlit night during the coyote episode, Tom walked the three quarters of a mile to where the carcass had been found. As he walked alone he was joined by John, Arte and Gwen, who silently escorted him along the moonlit deer trails that they had discovered. One by one, as they had joined him, they left him alone again to return to their new herd.

The end of December was also the last time that we saw Onray, the older of the whitetail. He had been keeping the company of the wild fawns. One of the fawns that were with the herd that Onray chose to travel with had a crooked ear that made him very easy to identify. This fawn and Onray were never seen again. We hoped that the herd had migrated down the stream that took Jessica to whitetail country. Perhaps by now Onray was part of her perfect little family.

20

HAPPY NEW YEAR

The New Year would bring us yet more challenges. I had still not gotten over the disappearances of our fawns during the summer. I don't think that night can ever again arrive without the thought of a mountain lion preying on my beloved fawns or llamas. Each morning brought a breath of relief as they were all accounted for.

The last few winters found us wintering fat little bear cubs. It was nice not to have to take care of any this year. The only thing that we had caged were Virgil and Virginia, the opossums that we didn't even know were around.

If I keep anything caged, I like it to have as much room as possible so the possums had the roomy space of the bear cage all to themselves. It was theirs only temporarily. About mid January a beaver trespassed into the city park zoo and was feasting on all the delicate plants and trees in their well manicured park. The zoo officials were not very pleased with the reconstruction that she was doing and wanted her relocated. Where do you relocate a beaver in the middle of the winter?

On a cold January night the beaver finally caught herself in the live trap set by Steve. He brought her up the next morning in a snowstorm. Virgil and Virginia were moved to another cage and the bear cage was prepared for the beaver. She was given a roomy den filled with straw in which she could hide, fresh willow branches, and a large tub of water. We were sure that she would be fine until spring.

Her nose had been rubbed raw as she fought the confines of the trap during the night. My heart ached for her as I tried to explain what was happening. We made a large Q-tip with a dowel and cotton and dabbed antibiotic cream on her raw sore face. She sought the quiet and safety of her shelter and hid her face in the corner. She needed time to rest after her terrible experience the night before.

The month of January brought very mild temperatures. Our weekends were spent relaxing from the hectic year that we had survived. Our two female llamas were getting more pregnant by the day. We were not sure when they were going to birth because we didn't know when they had been bred. The little male Zoom had impregnated them both; at least we were positive of that. We had assumed that he was too young but he proved us wrong.

Sunday morning, January twenty-seventh, I had gone to get a load of hay, and after unloading it we were going to take all the llamas for a walk. My plans were altered. While unloading the hay, I noticed that Lada was acting very irritable as the rest of the llamas watched me stack their food in the shelter of the barn. I went over to check on her and noticed that her water had already broken. It would only be a short time before we were the proud parents of another llama.

This was to be our first baby llama. I had never witnessed a birth before and was thankful that it was going to happen on a day that we were at home. By eleven-thirty she had given birth to a perfectly healthy little boy. "Nikita" was black except for a thin white mustache, and had all the qualities of a perfect llama. I was so excited that I took the next day off just to sit around and look at him. Surely Tyche would birth soon also.

The night that Nikita was born I received a phone call from Boulder, Colorado. Someone had shot and killed a mountain lion leaving four orphaned cubs. Would we take care of them if they could be captured? My thoughts of Nikita and Lada were replaced by the fear that I had experienced because of a mountain lion the past summer. Could I deal with that?

Nikita

The Wildlife officers were going to try to capture the orphans the next day and if they were successful they would let us know. My thoughts were very mixed about the situation. Would lion kittens attract older lions to our yard? Would our llamas and our deer be frightened? Did I really want to take this on? Question after question went on in my mind. I was thankful the next evening when they called and said that after an all day search they had found no clues to the whereabouts of the orphan cubs.

21

HERE KITTY, KITTY, KITTY

The next two weeks were spent enjoying the new llama and the eight remaining fawns. Nikita quickly got used to the fawns coming to visit him. He was now two weeks old and we were anxiously awaiting the birth of Tyke's baby. The beaver spent her days in her shelter and her nights out in the cage grooming and eating apples and carrots.

One warm afternoon Henrietta and I were sitting in the barn. We both kept hearing a strange sound coming from somewhere. Each time the sound occurred; Henry would lift her head and tilt her ears searching for the source of the sound. Finally it occurred to me that it was the beaver sound asleep and snoring inside her den. What a privilege to hear a beaver snore!

One Sunday morning in mid February I decided to plant some aspen trees in the yard. I spent the morning digging an enormous hole big enough for the three trees. Tom came out to show me an article in the Sunday newspaper. The head-line read, "Three Orphan Mountain Lions Captured after One killed By Car." I knew that by the end of the day we would have the three orphans to care for. Shortly after we read the article we received a call from the wildlife office. Arrangements were made to relay the kittens to us that afternoon.

While Tom was driving to pick up the lions, I stayed at home to move the beaver into the greenhouse. As I worked, questions about what I was about to face again tormented me. We would find the answers to all of my questions in the next three and a half months.

After I got the beaver moved I decided that I should get the trees in the hole that I had prepared before the deer came home and ate them. After getting the trees placed in the hole I began shoveling dirt and guess who magically appeared to help?

Having eight little deer helping you plant trees is quite an experience. They ate faster than I shoveled. Shoveling and shooing simultaneously I managed to get the trees in place and get a fence around them before they ate them. It took several tries to get them out of the fence before I could close it up. I know now what they mean when they say "Plant a Tree for Wildlife".

I had plenty of things to do while Tom was gone to keep my mind off what was about to happen. I would just have to take things as they came. Everything usually has a way of working out.

Tom arrived home with the three mountain lion kittens about 5:00 P.M. The sun had already set and none of the fawns were home at the time. We left the kittens in the carrier and set them inside the bear cage so they could come out when they were ready. It didn't take them long to come out of the carrier and run for the safety of the den at the rear of the cage. They had survived a long and trying day and were very hungry. With lots of mixed emotions I fed them a healthy serving of venison that they devoured the second I turned my back.

They had been on their own for the last two weeks. Their mother had been shot by a farmer because she was eating his chickens. The kittens had been trying to find food in a mountain community. They were even seen licking grease off backyard barbecue grills. After several unsuccessful attempts, the three were trapped by a resident in the community.

I had just spent the last six months living in fear of the very thing that was now living in triplicate in my barn. How much more ironic could things possibly be? My question of the deer being frightened was answered very shortly.

I saw our herd approaching the yard through the back. Donnie was in the lead as they came to the barn for their evening meal. The closer he came the puffier he got. With ears erect and hair standing on end he approached cautiously, sensing the predators now living in his barn. He bolted as he entered the barn, exhibiting the fear that I knew he would have. The others wouldn't come near the cage so I fed them in the yard. I was happy that they would at least stay to eat.

Over the next several days the fear of the mountain lions subsided. The deer seemed to know that they were a threat to their lives but under the circumstances they need not worry.

The day after we received the kittens the telephone wouldn't stop ringing. Suddenly we were celebrities. The cats had caused such a feeling of concern in the community in which they were captured that everyone wanted to follow up on them.

Kitty, Kitty, Kitty

It was bizarre! We have had hundreds of animals that no one ever cared about. Suddenly everyone wanted to pry into our personal lives. The television reporters were not very happy to be told that they were not welcome in our facility with their cameras and microphones. The lions were ours now and we would do what we had been entrusted to do, raise them and keep them wild. One television station even threatened to find our place using helicopters. Go ahead! Make my day!

We agreed to do a few telephone interviews with television and radio stations, but would in no way let anyone in to see the lions. We felt that it was only fair to let the concerned people know that the lions that they had become so fond of were being cared for in the best possible way.

The pressure was on. These three had to be a success. Lions had been getting a bad name because of an attack on a human just weeks before our three arrived. I'm sure that was the reason for all of the publicity they had gotten. They were ours now and every attempt would be made to make them dislike humans and avoid them at all costs.

The three kittens were beautiful. We estimated their weight to be about fifteen pounds. They were very elusive and would only peer out of the den if we were in the area and they knew that we could see them. Food was never taken in front of me, except for the very first feeding when they arrived half starved. When their empty little stomachs were filled, they would no longer take food if I were around.

They were very easy to care for. Cats are notoriously clean animals and used the very back corner of their den for their restroom. They kept themselves well groomed and clean by washing each other and rolling in the clean straw that lined their cage. They rarely left any food scraps and if they did it was buried meticulously with straw until consumed later.

Food consumption was tremendous. The Pueblo Nature Center was very helpful in giving us tons of venison and other wild meat to feed them. Twenty pounds of meat per day was a normal feeding.

We tried to give them as normal a diet as we possibly could. This meant picking up road kill on the highway on our way to and from work. We kept body bags in the car for this purpose. Both of us would scan the highway as Tom drove. He would slam on the brakes as I jumped out of the car to peel a freshly hit cottontail rabbit off the road and jump back in the car. Road kill was a special treat for the kittens. They ate everything. Occasionally they would save a piece of fur to play with when we weren't watching.

After about a week the media finally left us alone when we agreed to let one photographer come along on the release. When that would be no one seemed to know. It would depend on how fast the kittens grew. At the time of their arrival we assumed that they were between three and four months old. Within weeks the kittens had grown considerably and seemed to fit into the daily routine.

22

THE FIDDLER ON THE ROOF

Apple Betty, our wintering beaver, seemed quite happy living indoors. Her fondness for apples was the reason for her name. Another one of her favorite snacks was corn on the cob which happens to be quite expensive in the middle of the winter. Once a week I made a trip to the gravel pit a few miles from home and cut fresh willow and cottonwood branches for her to strip.

The fur on her face was growing back and she became more tolerant of us entering her living quarters. Some evenings we would just sit close to her and watch her groom and eat three or four ears of corn at fifty cents each. She would hold the corn by the ends with her manipulative little hands, strip one row of kernels, then rotate the ear and start on row two. It was like watching a typewriter.

She, just like Sweet Potato, would have house cleaning on a regular basis. When she decided to clean her house, it was an all night affair. The branches that she stripped were then placed in the door of her hide away. She would be with us until the ponds thawed late in the spring. Apple Betty would then join Sweet Potato's colony.

Everything again seemed to be going smoothly. Everyone had gotten used to the mountain lions living with us and most of the fears that I had about keeping them had disappeared. Shortly after the arrival of the kittens Steve called me at work one afternoon and asked us to pick up a raccoon that had been attacked by dogs. When we arrived at the wildlife office we were greeted by a snarling, mad, but not too severely injured young raccoon.

We decided that the best thing to do would be to give it a nice quiet place to hide and feel sorry for itself and in a few days release her in a remote area. The raccoon seemed glad to have some food and a good place to hide. It growled and tried to attack every time I approached the cage.

A few days later, while the coon was climbing the cage wires, I noticed that a band of fur about four inches wide right above her tail had been worn almost to the skin. Someone had been keeping her in a very small enclosure for quite some time. No wonder she was so agitated. The person who had been keeping her had evidently tormented and teased her until that was all that she knew. She expected it.

We decided to let her out of her cage to see what she would do. She thought it was wonderful, so much freedom, so many things to look at, so many things to touch. She spent the afternoon and evening climbing in the rafters in the barn and walking on the roofs of all the outbuildings.

I wondered what she would do when night time came. She had a choice now. She was no longer confined to a space that would rub the hair off her body. She could go wherever she chose. She just happened to choose to live on our roof for the next four and a half months.

Our three story house is all rough cut pine and quite easy for a raccoon to climb. A tall Russian Olive tree was her staircase to the roof that edges our surveillance deck. In the morning I found her huddled in the corner of the deck trying to sleep. Before we left for work I took a wooden shelter, a bowl of water, a blanket, and food to her. The southern exposure made it a terrific place to spend the winter. She became known as Fiddler. When anyone asked about her we simply replied, "Oh, Fiddler? Well, she's on the roof."

Fiddler was obviously accustomed to being around humans. She was not the least bit shy about climbing on us and fondling us any way that she wanted to. It was perfectly okay for her to frisk our pockets, or rotate our eyeballs and floss our teeth with her sensitive little hands, but look out if we tried to touch her. Her body was strictly off limits to human hands. She seemed highly frustrated and unfortunately took out all of her frustrations on us and our house.

Tom has subdivided raccoons into two categories: air coons and ground coons. Vidal was a ground coon. She never climbed the house or played much in the rafters in the barn. Fiddler, however, was definitely an air coon. We very seldom saw her on the ground. She was always peering at us from somewhere up above.

One day when I was changing clothes after work I opened the bedroom door that leads out to a deck on the second story of the house. I noticed that the screen on the outer door was bent and just kind of hanging there ready to fall out. I thought that the wind had something to do with it and told Tom that it needed to be fixed. The next afternoon I heard terrible noises between the door and the screen door. When I opened the inner door I came face to face with Fiddler sitting very comfortably in the diamond shapes that once had screen covering them.

The screen was shredded, the frame was bent beyond recognition, and I realized that the wind was not a factor in the mutilated screen door. I caught her in the act and there was absolutely nothing that I could do about it. I would have been a total fool to try to stop her, so I quickly slammed the inner door and let her finish what she had started. Tom had to put the glass window back in the door frame. This stopped her break and entry tactics.

A few days later I was going out the back door and when I opened it, I came face to face with her again. Since she couldn't come in the bedroom she would try another entry. This time we successfully got her out of the door by dousing her with a glass of water before she could do much damage.

We still had one more screen door and quickly put the glass in it before she found it. She gave up trying to break into the house and found a new game. Since all the screens on the house were gone she found the one on the large door to the greenhouse and ripped a hole in it, just to prove that she could. Now I had to be extra careful not to leave the outer door open when she was around.

Fiddler had her days and nights mixed up. Most raccoons sleep all day and prowl all night. Not Fidd. She got up when I did and came off the roof to pester me while I did my chores before we left for work. After work we were met by her and pestered until we all retired for the night. She would climb the tree, cross the roof and sleep the night away in her rooftop shelter.

One night I went out to the greenhouse to check on something and didn't pay attention to the door. In the morning I put the cat in the greenhouse and noticed that things seemed to be somewhat disrupted. The sacks of grain and sunflower seed were open and their contents scattered all over the floor. The cat food dish was in the middle of the room. Tom's kites were scattered everywhere. A box containing five hundred bullets had been opened and the bullets were evenly distributed among the tools in each drawer of a large tool box, but I couldn't hear a thing.

It really wasn't too difficult to figure out what had happened. I knew that she still had to be in there somewhere, but where? Mumbling to myself and picking things up, I heard noises in the loft of the room. I climbed the ladder and came face to face with the culprit. Now the problem was how do we get her out of here?

Fiddler seemed to identify with Tom more than me so he came in to see if he could get her out without too big of an ordeal. She liked it in there and had no intention of leaving until she decided that it was time. Tom finally had to get the noose pole and evict the screaming, snarling coon. Fiddler gave Tom the cold shoulder for at least three days afterward.

The night before when I went out to the greenhouse, Fiddler slipped in the door without my knowing and had the time of her life. The only courteous thing that she had accomplished during her escapade was to relieve herself in the cat litter box. Now we had four doors to guard plus some first level windows that she had discovered.

I guess she finally gave up on the idea of breaking in and found other things to focus her attention on, like pestering the llamas. Fiddler would entertain them by doing acrobatic routines through the bars on the fence panels dividing their pastures.

They would gather around and watch in amazement as she twirled and spun and hung on by one hand. She would then lean over backward, weave herself through the bars to the top and pose as if waiting for them to hold up their scorecards. We really couldn't blame her for her behavior. She was simply enjoying the freedom that she had waited for so long.

23

SPRING IS IN THE AIR

We were still anxiously awaiting the birth of our second baby llama. Nikita was already a month old and growing like a weed. Tyche was getting sick of me following her around and staring at her behind as though I didn't think that she knew what she was doing. By the first of March I knew that it would be very soon.

On March fourth, a Monday morning, the first thing I did was go out to the llama pen to check on her. I knew the minute I saw her that today would be the day. Our teaching contract provides us with two days a year that we can take off for personal reasons. I rushed indoors to call off for the day, sent Tom on his way, gathered up all necessary birthing items and went outside to wait.

I had pestered her enough and decided to keep my distance and interfere only if it were necessary. My heart was pounding when I saw her water break and the tiny black head gasp its first breath. Twenty minutes later Tyche had given birth to a multicolored little girl whom we named Tiah. Within minutes she was nursing and able to stand and walk around.

Nikita was thrilled with his new little companion and all the other llamas gathered around to see her. The long wait was over. I couldn't wait for Tom to get home. The best thing about having the two babies was that their mothers, not I, had to nurse them.

Except for the severe cold snap at Christmas the winter was very mild. As spring was approaching I knew that it would not be long before Apple Betty could be released. She didn't seem unhappy; she was eating at least four ears of corn a day, plus several apples and newly sprouted cottonwood and willow branches.

The fawns and the wild deer, including Big Tim, were still coming to the yard to feed. Some nights I thought I would have to put up a "Take a Number Station" for entering and leaving the barn to eat hay. The mountain lion kittens were fascinated with the parade of deer walking by their cage. Fiddler loved to walk on top of their cage and torment them. Surely she would not have been this stupid if she knew that they could get her.

Tim still had his antlers from the year before and I hoped that he would loose at least one in our yard. About the middle of March we noticed that he had finally shed his antlers and I searched, but did not find them anywhere near the yard. I was, however, fortunate enough to find one of them while riding my mountain bike between the ridges where the deer spend much of their time. I knew it was his because the tip of one of the tines was broken.

After he shed his antlers, he took refuge with the eight fawns. I had read that when a buck drops his antlers, he may try to hide among a herd of does or young deer. I witnessed this very thing happening right in our yard.

As evening approached the fawns would come out of the oak to feed. Only now there were nine. Camouflaged in the line of fawns was Big Tim, hunkered down trying to get to their level. It was really funny. We could almost feel what he was doing. "I'm a fawn, I'm a fawn. You can't bother me." He did this for several weeks. Finally, as the new antler growth began to emerge, he left to join the older crowd.

Henrietta was still watching over Donnie. As the others would leave for the day, Henrietta would remain faithful and stay home to baby sit. Occasionally, she would con Artie into giving her a break and he would take over for her. There was always someone to watch over the little buck. It wouldn't be long before he would start to travel with them. He would know when he could keep up.

24

RUFUS THE RED FOX

The past year had been one of the busiest years that we had gone through since we began wildlife rehabilitation more than ten years ago. The feeling of accomplishment was still there even with the losses that we suffered from our disappearing fawns. Spring time was right around the corner which meant the arrival of newborn creatures would soon begin. Our spring vacation was the last week in March and we were looking forward to spending a lot of time with the new llamas and just relaxing before the season began.

The first day of vacation brought us a tiny orphan red fox whose eyes had not yet opened. Rufus came from the city of Lamar that is about one hundred and fifty miles east of us. The game warden from that area has managed to get the United States Mail trucks to relay orphans to us. This saves hours of driving time for him and for us. The drivers are already on a strict schedule and there is never any problem with anyone being too early or too late.

In the past we have received various animals in this manner. One driver had the pleasure of delivering five baby raccoons the previous year. He felt that the back of the semi was too hot for the coons and allowed them to ride up front with him in the air conditioned cab.

Rufus arrived via U.S. mail, a fluffy ball of brown fuzz with a tiny white tip on the end of his two inch tail, which identified him as a red fox. Being this young, he required four hour feedings. The little fox readily took the milk offered to him in a pet nurser bottle. They are very easy to care for when they are this small. All that their little bodies require are nutrition, safety and warmth. The mischief comes later.

Rufus arrived on the very first day of our break. It gave us a chance to get him established and to learn his needs before returning to work. His eyes opened the second day that we had him. Once their eyes are open they begin to experiment with eating on their own. It was only a couple of days before the little fox was eating his meals of baby food and milk from a saucer.

He quickly outgrew the intensive care cage and was moved to a larger cage that we kept in the house. We felt comfortable leaving him during the day since he was able to eat all by himself. At night we would let the little fox out of his cage to play on our living room couch that is covered with stuffed animal toys.

Roofie also had his own collection of private friends that he rough housed with while we were not around. His favorite was a stuffed, pink, baby aardvark. The aardvark was twice as large as he was but he managed to carry it around without too much trouble. He took out all his aggression on the poor thing. I would hate to guess how often he "killed" aardvark while practicing the skills he would need in the future. He would straddle the stuffed toy, grab it behind the neck, growl and shake it back and forth, until he was sure it was dead. In a matter of just a few weeks Roofie outgrew his indoor cage and we moved him into the intensive care room in the greenhouse, the same room where Gracie had learned to hunt mice. At night we would bring him indoors to play with us and his couch friends until we went to bed.

Roofie liked to hide everything that was special to him, behind the toilet in the downstairs bathroom. One evening I heard Tom's laughter coming from the bathroom. He heard something and around the cabinet came Roofie, wrestling with his prized aardvark, to add to the stash already accumulated behind the toilet.

As Roofie got older, I knew that it wouldn't be very long until he would not be able to play inside anymore. Nothing was safe. He was starting to play havoc with my plants and soon discovered the stairs to the second floor. The permanent move to the greenhouse was made easier with the arrival of Roofie's sibling sister. Roofie was picked up on the shoulder of a highway after his mother was killed by a passing car. Their den was just a short distance from the road. Someone else had found his sister and had tried to keep her as a pet. It was very coincidental that she arrived about the same time that Roof was becoming such a pest.

The people had discovered that foxes were not such great house pets and became upset when they could not train her by slapping her with newspapers when she urinated on their carpet or bit their three year old when he tried to play with her.

They decided to do what they should have done from the beginning which was to notify the Division of Wildlife.

The timing was perfect. The U.S. mail delivered a package for Roofie. It was his sister and they instantly became best friends. I didn't feel as bad now about not letting him in the house to play. Her arrival made it a lot easier for all of us. The two brought back memories of Gracie and George, the pair of red foxes that we had raised two years ago.

These two, however, did not live in the greenhouse as long as Gracie and George had. Roofie and his sister, Roofieanne, were eager to move outdoors before school was dismissed for the summer. They chose to set up residence under a small shed next to the barn. I was glad that they chose to move outdoors so soon. I certainly didn't miss cleaning up after them like I had done with George and Gracie.

25

GOODBYE APPLE BETTY

The warm spring temperatures signaled the time for Apple Betty to move on to better surroundings. About mid April she made the same trip that Sweet Potato had eight months earlier.

As we drove to the area I was very excited to see what Sweet Potato's colony had accomplished during the past fall and winter. There had been only one large pond the previous year. The colony had since moved upstream and successfully stopped the flow of the stream to create another fairly large pond.

As we walked around the new pond, I felt privileged to have personally known one of the construction workers on the project. We released Apple Betty at the lower pond so that she could introduce herself gradually to the occupying colony.

We set her carrier on the shore line and she slid out and into the pond within seconds. We watched her for only minutes before she found the entry to the lodge and vanished inside.

Everyone had seemed pessimistic about keeping a beaver through the winter. She had been very accommodating and quite entertaining. She managed just fine on her diet of corn on the cob, apples and assorted branches.

By the time that she was released there was no indication that she had been injured at all. Her raw, scraped face had healed perfectly and the trust that she had given us was a true compliment. Now she was free again. We gave her a second chance at life. At least here she would not get herself in trouble by damaging someone's prized duck pond. We left with a wonderful feeling. We were not taking away; we were returning something, something that has a very special place on this earth and in our hearts.

26

PLEASE DON'T LET HIM DIE

I guess I live in a fantasy world. The things that go on daily in our yard are things that most people would pay to witness. Every day is special. There is always one or more of our creatures around to share very special moments with. Usually they are happy times, but sometimes they are very troublesome. A day never goes by without something special happening. Evenings and mornings are always the busiest.

All of the fawns were still accounted for although some of them were becoming much more independent. Donnie, being the youngest, was still spending much time around home. He was starting to roam with the others now and I knew that he was finally growing up.

One evening about the middle of May, all the fawns had left for the night except Donnie. That wasn't unusual but when I went to bid him good night I could tell that he was feverish. It concerned me but not overly so. In the morning Donnie came to the porch shortly after everyone else. I could tell that he was not feeling good but he was eating and left through the pasture for the day.

I thought about him all day and nervously awaited their arrival that evening. All of the fawns came except Donnie. I was beginning to get scared. He still had not come home by morning. I knew that he had gone off by himself and had probably died. I had seen it many times before. Once they get sick it is very unusual for them to get well again. I tried to be optimistic. After all Marco had been gone for eleven days and he had come home.

After three days we had started to loose hope. We began looking for flocks of magpies or crows that would tell us where he had chosen to die. On Friday we drove into the yard and could see a large flock of crows about a hundred yards across the pasture. Without speaking we both got out of the car and solemnly walked toward them. They were only eating seeds from the ground. There was no sign of Donnie. We headed toward the house and I stopped to visit with the llamas as Tom went to unlock the house.

As he walked to the door, I heard him say, "Cec, Donnie is over here." I ran toward the house and saw the little buck curled up under the deck looking very miserable. His eyes were pasted shut with mucous as were both of his nostrils which severely restricted his breathing. He was also very hot to the touch.

Without changing clothes we began doctoring him. He hadn't died after all, but he definitely was very sick and knew where to come for help. His temperature was high but not extreme. As I cleared his eyes and nose with a warm wet towel Tom administered a shot of antibiotics. Donnie took a big drink of cold water and a few bites of grain and apples and found a cool shady place to lie down and rest. I didn't want to pester him but checked on him often. At dusk Donnie went to the barn to spend the night.

At nightfall we gathered up a few blankets and bedded down with him in the straw. He seemed to appreciate someone being close to him just for security. Fiddler was now changing to a night routine and spent much of her time in the barn. I did not feel comfortable leaving the sick little buck alone in the barn with her.

We were relieved that Donnie had come home and had no trouble falling off to sleep. I don't know what time it was when we were awakened by not one, but two raccoons. Vidal had come for a visit and had finally met Fiddler. Why did it have to be on a night that we had chosen to sleep in their territory?

The air and ground coon philosophy held true. Fiddler stayed in the rafters and snarled at Vidal who was down on the ground with us. Tom was so sound asleep that he didn't even feel Vidal searching through his pockets. Neither of the two raccoons bothered sick little Donnie.

In the morning we all felt better. Donnie came out and ate and drank and spent the rest of the day in the shade of the scrub oak. Hopefully the antibiotics would help him fight his illness. The next night Donnie decided to stay in the oak brush.

I hated to have the vulnerable deer out alone at night. Again we gathered blankets and pillows and burrowed in with him. It was a bit crowded in the bushes and about eleven o'clock Tom decided to go inside to sleep.

Donnie and I fell fast asleep until I was awakened by Henrietta busily chewing on my blanket and Fiddler examining my pillow. I looked around and saw that Donnie had awakened and left. The two had obviously pestered him before they started on me and he was smart enough to leave. I was getting my fill of them and decided that I would do the same.

I crawled out of the bushes with my pillow, blanket and flashlight and decided to join Tom. Before going inside I went to look in the barn and sure enough, there was Donnie, sound asleep in the straw. I changed my mind about going indoors and joined him again. We both slept until morning without any intruders.

By Sunday evening Donnie seemed a little better. The antibiotics must have been helping. He was eating more and was less congested. He looked terrible. The little buck looked as though he had been in a concentration camp. You could see his ribs and the bones of his spine. His coat looked awful with the white spots of his childhood now sticking out in black patches. Would he ever look like a real deer?

Another night in the barn wouldn't hurt. Again we curled up together next to the opossum cage with the lion cage at our feet. The night started very peacefully. The first time I was awakened was by a skunk fight just above our heads. Luckily the spray missed us and the breeze carried the fumes out of the barn.

Virgil and Virginia, the opossums who had spent almost a year never more than two inches apart, were now pacing and feeling the spring weather. Possums can make some pretty strange sounds and would soon have to be set free. I made that decision the second time I awoke.

That night the cats were anything but inhibited. I guess they couldn't see us well enough to care. During the night they played "elk" ball. A huge portion of their supper had been saved for midnight playtime. They tossed and batted the hunk of meat around and occasionally stopped to rip some hair out. At least they were getting their exercise.

"What else could happen?" I thought to myself. It didn't take long to find out. After the "elk" ball game, we settled down only to be awakened by little hands massaging my hair and scalp. Vidal was back and was into hairstyling. At least she was gentle. The air coon was in the rafters voicing her opinion of Vidal's presence. I was glad that Donnie was feeling better. I don't think I could have taken another night on the barn floor.

Donnie seemed to improve daily. We kept him on antibiotics for several more days and his symptoms were slowly disappearing. He was truly a miracle. By the end of May the little buck had finally shed his terrible, scraggly coat, gained several pounds and was beginning to look like a real deer. Even his stubby antlers began to grow again.

27

STARS FOR A DAY

The beginning of May brought back many memories. One morning as I was dressing for work I heard Tom say in a very excited voice, "Look across the road!" Three bull elk and one cow elk were standing there staring into our yard.

Larry would be three years old now and about the size of the three gazing quizzically into our yard. I had never seen elk this close to the house before, except Larry. Had he returned to show his herd where he had grown up? The four casually walked the fence line and one seemed especially interested. When he lived here there were only two of those strange looking animals with the funny hair, now there were seven. As they slowly went on their way over the horizon, three disappeared and one lingered, still reminiscing his childhood.

Suddenly he realized that the others were leaving and in his jerky elk stride trotted off to join them. I knew that it was Larry. There was no way to be absolutely positive but the feeling that I had inside assured me that it was. There are some things that you just know.

We had finally received word that the mountain lion kittens would be released on May twenty ninth. It was time for them to go. The three had lost their baby teeth and had become young adults.

We felt very successful about keeping them so wild. They were simply fed and kept clean. No attempts were ever made to try to make them feel comfortable around us or to trust us in anyway. The closeness that we usually develop with our animal friends was never attempted with the lions. I have a great deal of respect for them and what they are capable of doing. They were ready to make it on their own.

Kitty, Kitty, Kitty, as they were called, would be tranquilized, ear tagged and moved to a very remote area of the state. I really was tired of hauling out buckets of bloody meat and splattered rabbits to them everyday. They would have to feed themselves now.

We had been successful about keeping out the media and the curiosity seekers during the three and a half months that they were with us. One game warden, a still photographer, and a video cameraman would cover the release with us.

The day of their departure went very smoothly. Steve and Tom, using jab poles, professionally tranquilized the cats after they were isolated in the den of their cage. They went to sleep within minutes of being shot. After they were asleep they were weighed, ear tagged, and measured. We also checked their teeth and their claws and sexed them.

The entire time that the cats were with us I had wondered what sex they were and what it would feel like to touch them. Now that they were asleep I could run my hands through their luxurious fur, look into their eyes, and feel their powerful muscles. They were spectacular. From a weight of fifteen pounds at their arrival they had each gained at least forty pounds. The largest was a male who now weighed sixty-three pounds. The other two were females. During the checkout time I was able to make clay imprints of their paws that will always be treasured keepsakes.

The mountain lions were then loaded into a bear trap for their journey back to the wild. The drive to the release area took us five hours. Two and a half of those hours were on four wheel drive roads. The object was to get them as far away as possible from human contact.

We arrived at the release site about 5:00 P.M. The lions were now awake and sensed what was about to happen. The trap was backed into a beautiful meadow and as we stood back to watch, the game warden raised the door to free the lions.

One by one they sprang from the enclosure and bounded gracefully through the meadow into the security of the surrounding trees. It was the first time in three and a half months that the lions could again experience the freedom of running. They disappeared before we could catch our breath.

A release such as the one we had just witnessed is the reason that we do what we do. To see something that was born to be free, held captive for various reasons, and then allowed their freedom again is something that cannot be described. You can only feel it in your heart.

The day had been long and very stressful, but we had accomplished what we had set out to do. It was as though a part of us had gone with them, a part of us, too, had been released. We felt great.

The television stations were anxious to get the footage of the lion release. Radio and newspapers were also vying for the news. The next day on our way to work we stopped for a newspaper. There in full color on the front page of the Denver Post was a picture of Tom and Steve measuring the adolescent lions. The next few days we basked in the glory of being media stars. We really are not publicity seekers but I must admit that it made both of us feel pretty special.

28

THE "E" WORD

Steve, our game warden and good friend, is always joking with me by saying that he is bringing us some strange animal. He is very convincing and though there is a doubt in my mind, I usually believe him.

Last year he called and told me that he was bringing us elk twins. "Sure Steve, bring them up" I said. I knew he was kidding, wasn't he? Maybe not! Oh God! "Where are we going to put them?" I didn't know whether to believe him or not. He finally convinced me that he would be up with the twins within the next hour and hung up the phone.

Tom was on his way out the door to figure out someplace to put the big babies while I called the wildlife office. Lee answered the phone and I could tell by her voice that the two of them were having a good laugh. We really were relieved but would never have turned them down. Since the "elk joke" we have all referred to elk as "E's". "Don't say the "E" word", we would laugh. It could mean that you will be getting one.

On May thirty first, just two days after the lions were released; Steve called us about 9:00 P.M. A cow elk had been killed on the highway. The motorist who witnessed the accident reported that a calf had been seen with the elk that was killed. The game warden went back to the area with his elk call and was able to get the calf to come to him. He then relayed the baby to Steve who relayed her to us. We picked up "E"dith Ann about midnight and brought her home.

It seemed ironic that the lions were released in the same part of the state that the little cow elk was from. One of the reasons this area had been chosen for the release was because newborn calves and fawns were abundant there. The large baby that was now in our possession would not be prey for the lions.

We brought the carrier containing the big baby into the house for the night. She didn't understand the bottle but drank her milk from a bowl and settled down as all babies this young usually do. In the morning Edith drank her milk and we moved her to the intensive care room. By the next feeding she had learned to nurse from a bottle.

The weekend that Edith arrived was the three day Memorial Day Holiday. After the holiday we would have to return to work until June sixth. Since we were not at home during the day, we decided to leave her in the room, just to be safe. Edith didn't mind a bit. She was very content with her nice cool, quiet room. She was fed before we left for work, when we got home at four in the afternoon and then again about 11:00 P.M.

We couldn't wait for school to be out for the summer. My only hope was that this summer would be more relaxed than last. The week flew by and the sixth of June was a day of celebration. It was my birthday, school was out for the summer, and I had my very own smiling cow elk. The timing was perfect. Edith was ready to begin outdoor excursions. I wondered how last years fawns would react to her. There were still several who made frequent appearances, especially Donnie and Henrietta.

On the first day of vacation, Edith was fed in her room and then allowed to follow me outdoors to get acquainted. The yearlings must have known that we were having a coming out party. Donnie, Henrietta, Artie, John and Felipe had gathered to meet Edith Ann. They all greeted her and welcomed her to the orfawnage. She thought they were all wonderful and smiled at all of them.

Edith & Donny

As the group grazed around the yard, Edith followed them until she got tired and then she laid down by the pinion tree to rest. As she nestled in the tall grass, Felipe, our remaining white tail buck, washed her face and ears until she was wet. Edith remained in the yard as the yearlings left for the day. That was the last time that we saw Felipe. Perhaps he was telling Edith what to expect at her new home. The beautiful yearling buck had made the decision to move on to whitetail country.

Edith was allowed to stay outdoors until sunset when she willingly followed me back into her room, was fed and settled down until morning. I hadn't fed her outside yet and wondered how Donnie was going to react to someone else getting a bottle. It had not been that long ago that he was weaned. Sure enough, Donnie thought that he too should have a bottle. Just for fun I let him try but he had lost the ability to nurse. Now when Edith had her bottle outdoors, Donnie was served a bowl of apples to keep him from pestering her while she ate.

29

EDITH'S LITTLE FRIENDS

June twelfth brought Edith some friends that were her own age. The two were approximately the same age as she but nowhere near her size. Another sculptured whitetail doe came to us from Rocky Ford, Colorado. Someone had picked her up and had taken her to the vet. The vet then contacted the wildlife officer and he had her relayed to us. The little doe was in perfect shape (most whitetails are perfect) and surely should have been left alone. The damage had already been done, however, and now she was ours to raise. Edith was in the yard when she came and welcomed her by licking her. The little doe was then fed and left to rest in the intensive care room.

Later in the day another fawn had been found on the side of a highway near Canon City, Colorado. The little mule doe, less than one week old, had a broken leg. Tourists from Missouri had found her and taken her to the Forest Service Office. That office then called the Wildlife Office who told them to call us.

The tourists were very concerned about the little doe and were glad that they had found someone who was willing to take care of her. They wanted to help any way that they possibly could. I had them take her to a veterinarian who had helped me out a few years earlier with another fawn.

While they were taking her to the doctor, I called and asked him to look at her and do whatever he needed to do. I would be there within twenty minutes to pick her up and pay for whatever needed to be done. He agreed.

When I entered the waiting room, I was met by a family of at least six. One of the teenagers was cradling the injured little doe as the rest hovered around softly talking to her. They placed the fawn in my outstretched arms as we visited. They knew that the little doe was going to be well cared for and felt very satisfied that they were able to help.

I took her out to the carrier in my truck and then returned inside to take care of the bill. Knowing that we are not reimbursed for any of our expenses, the vet refused to charge me any fee. He had set her leg because he cared. I will always remember him for that.

Now the perfect little whitetail would have company to share the privacy of her room. The new little doe was introduced to the whitetail and they became Deer Ann and Deer Abby. The two little fawns would stay in the intensive care room for at least a week. When they become curious and begin to move around more after feeding, it is an indication that it is time for them to move outdoors where they can begin eating natural food.

Deer Ann would be in her cast for three weeks. The stiff cast on her right rear leg didn't seem to slow her down at all. In fact, of the two she was the most curious and the first to want to leave the room and explore the greenhouse.

Edith was at the stage where she was spending her days in the yard and returning inside for the night. What was she going to think of her roommates? Edith weighed about fifty pounds. Deer Ann and Deer Abby weighed about four pounds each.

At dusk I fed Edith outdoors and took her inside. When she entered the room the two little ones instantly popped up to see her. Both of them ran under her and tried to nurse. Edith just looked down at them curiously. When they finally figured out that she wasn't going to give them any milk, they returned to their beds in the straw.

I remembered the feeling that I had when Larry and Jessica were confined in a small area. I just knew that he was going to squash her. I was again facing a similar situation. Only Edith had two of them to squash and one already had a broken leg.

I sat in the corner of the room and watched to see what was going to happen. Edith walked over to them and bent down to nuzzle and lick them. Then she carefully maneuvered around them and lay down between her two new friends with a look of contentment on her face.

The summer had started gradually and I decided that I was not going to stress myself out. I was going to take one day at a time and try not to worry myself sick over things that I had no control over. I tried to condition myself to relax more and enjoy what was going on around me. I decided that if God gave me an elk to raise, he certainly would not deluge me with fourteen fawns. At least I hoped that he wouldn't.

Edith drank as much milk at one feeding as four fawns would have consumed. She was the first one fed in the morning. She was not as pushy as Larry had been and drank her bottles in a very lady like manner. After eating she would rather go off with Donnie than hang around and chew on me.

After Edith ate, I went in the intensive care room to feed Deer Ann and Deer Abby and then waited until they settled down. I actually had time to sit on the front porch and share a bowl of cereal with Rufie and Rufieanne. As we ate, Fiddler would tease the foxes or play chase with Edith Ann around the pinion trees and the scrub oak.

One morning, after breakfast, I was inside washing bottles when I heard Tom say, "Look, three Men and a Baby!" Pictured in the large kitchen window were Donnie, John and Artie with Edith Ann smiling happily in the midst of the resting trio.

30

VIRGIL AND VIRGINIA GET DIVORCED

During the last several weeks Virgil and Virginia were no longer snuggling and sleeping together. They spent most of their time in opposite corners of the cage. I knew that it was time for Virgil and Virginia Opossum to be released, but I was unsure where to locate them. I didn't want to just open their cage and let them free themselves because the foxes lived so close. Foxes love to torment and tease everything that moves and I didn't want them harassing the two. I couldn't take them somewhere and just leave them because they had been so dependent on us for the last year. They needed to work out gradually.

I finally decided to take them, their house and food and water up to the pole barn where we had last seen Larry. It was only a short walk through the llama pasture and I could check on them periodically. Late one afternoon, in the first part of June, we drove the two to their new home. We camouflaged their house in the scrub oak, left a big bowl of water and some food and hoped that they would be gone when we returned to check.

Virgil & Virginia

Later that evening I walked up to see if they were still around. I really didn't expect either of them to leave their house until dark, but Virginia was nowhere to be seen. Virgil was still sound asleep inside. I knew he would be gone in the morning.

Early the next day I again walked through the pasture to see if Virgil had received the call of the wild. A little more than half way there, I met Virgil coming down the deer path toward home. I tried to pick him up but the fifty teeth in his mouth told me that I ought to leave him alone. I grabbed him by his long rat tail and carted him back to his house at the pole barn. For the next several days I checked on him in the morning and in the evening. I was actually stupid enough to keep taking him food. No wonder he wouldn't leave.

Finally the evening came when I went to check on him and he wasn't in his house. The food I had left the evening before was still in his bowl and he was nowhere in sight. At least he had the opportunity to leave at his own speed, very slowly. The next morning I was out in the tall grasses behind the house foraging for choice dandelions to feed the tiny cottontail bunnies that we were raising at the time.

Something in the grass moved and startled me. When I parted the grass to see what it was I looked straight into the face of Virgil and his fifty tooth grin. "Okay, Virgil," I said. "if you want to live here, fine. There's the barn, make yourself at home." He did. At least until he decided that it was time to move on.

I would find him burrowed between the bales of hay and even in his wooden house that I had moved back into the barn. It took him awhile, but he finally made up his mind and left. For all that I know he may still be living somewhere close by. It wouldn't surprise me a bit to move something and find the fat, toothy Virgil.

31

SPECIAL DELIVERY

Over the last several years we have received fawns from various parts of the state. The hardiest seem to come from Lamar, Colorado, which is about one hundred and fifty miles east of us. Some of the deer that we have raised from this town are Big Tim, Big Doe and big burly John Deer. The game warden from the area is very proud when I tell him that he has the toughest deer in the state.

On June twenty-first the officer called and asked if we had room for another fawn. If we didn't have room we would make some. After a lengthy discussion on how he was going to relay her to us, I suggested that he do what he does with the orphan raccoons, foxes and other small animals. Put her on the U.S. Mail truck. Why not? When contained in a quiet carrier they make the journey quite well. It really wouldn't be any different than traveling by car. Arrangements were made with the driver and Tom intercepted the truck and picked her up.

Three fawns in the intensive care room would be a bit crowded. When the new fawn arrived we decided that it was time to move outdoors. Ann, Abby and the new doe were moved to the outdoor pen the next morning.

As usual the new little doe from Lamar was larger, but not any older than the other two. When they chased each other and played she acted like a little tank, mowing down everything in her way. One evening, during playtime, she knocked Annie down and I looked at her and said, "Be careful! You're like a bull-dozer." The name rang a bell inside my head. From then on she became known as Doezer.

Edith was now living outdoors. She was very dependent on Donnie and some of the other yearlings that still made occasional appearances. I was afraid that she would try to follow them when they left and I didn't think that she was old enough to be going very far.

One evening she followed them as they left for the night. She managed to get herself through the fence and disappeared. I tried to call her back, but her mind had been made up and I was not going to change it. About thirty minutes later I heard a pathetic squealing coming from across the road. Edith appeared on the horizon heading for home. Her friends managed to ditch her and she got scared. I watched as she maneuvered her large body through the fence and ran to the security of her little friends in the pen. Edith decided that she would wait at home for her older friends. They seem to know when it is time to explore further horizons.

One morning Tom left in his truck to go into the pasture to do some wood cutting. I stayed at home until I thought that everyone had bedded down for the day. I then started to ride my bicycle over to help him load the cut wood.

As I started up the road, Donnie saw me leaving and started to come along. Edith saw us and thought that she could come also, after all her surrogate mother would be with her. I tried to discourage the two, but couldn't get rid of them. When I reached the top of the hill, I stopped to look back and could see yet another deer in the yard staring up the road at us. In a matter of minutes, Henrietta joined our group and we went to look for Tom.

As Tom and I loaded the wood into his truck, the three of them grazed and then laid down in the shade until we were finished. When I was ready to leave, I got on my bicycle and the three of them followed me home. I'll never forget that day. When we got home the three vanished into the scrub oak until dusk.

It was now the latter part of June and the summer was off to a wonderful start. Annie, Abby, and Doezer were thriving and would soon be able to leave the pen for the day.

32

MIDGEY

On June twenty-seventh, Tom made a trip to a nearby town to rescue four baby skunks after their mother was killed. Most people aren't very sympathetic with the aromatic black and white creatures, but the people who found the skunks were very concerned about what was going to happen to them. Tom assured them that we had a special place in our hearts for the little varmints and that they would be given a good home. The four orphans increased our skunk population to five. We already had one who would appreciate the company.

Since no one was living in the intensive care room I let the litter stay in there. I made a burrow for them using a large comforter. They were able to eat by themselves which made them very easy to keep. None of them were crazy about humans and although they weighed about six ounces each they didn't hesitate to threaten us by stomping their front feet and aiming their small round bottoms at us with their tails sticking straight up. Even at this age they are capable of spraying anything that happens to upset them.

Later that same day the game warden from a nearby town brought us a fawn that two young boys had been caring for after she had been injured. The boys had rescued the fawn from a hayfield that was being cut. I noticed a clean white bandage around her back hoof as I carried her into the intensive care room. Jake, the game warden said that the boys told him that she was cut and that they had kept the wound clean and bandaged.

As I sat with the fawn in my lap to inspect her injury, Jake sat quietly in the corner of the room. I carefully took the wrap off expecting a superficial cut. A lump formed in my throat when I saw that her whole foot, up to the first joint, had been severed. I looked at Jake who quietly said, "It's not fair, is it?" No it isn't fair, something this innocent, this vulnerable, should not have to begin life this way.

I didn't want to think about it now. We would deal with it when it was necessary. Now she needed to be fed and get some rest. The tiny doe was named Midgey because of her petite size and seemed very content staying in the intensive care room with the five little skunks.

In just a couple of days we decided that Midgey could go out to the pen with Doezer, Annie and Abby. Her foot was padded and bandaged to stay clean. She was able use the leg though it was a little shorter than the other three. I knew that something would eventually have to be done with the leg. After talking with the vet we decided to wait until she was older and stronger.

She was marvelous about letting me change the bandage every few days. She would sit in my lap and nuzzle my ear as I cleaned, medicated and rewrapped her leg. When I was finished she would bounce off to be with her friends. As I watched her I often thought to myself, "Why can't humans deal with tragedy the way the animal world can?"

33

THINGS ARE "DOE'ING VERY WELL

By this time last summer we hadn't been able to catch our breath. My prayers really had been answered. We were having a much slower year. Usually in July we don't seem to have a day without something coming in. A whole week had gone by with no new arrivals.

Edith and the fawns were doing well. We took Annie's cast off and it was as though nothing had ever happened to her. Edith was about the most undemanding creature we have ever had. All that she asked of us was her eight bottles of milk in the morning and again in the evening. The rest of the time she didn't have much to do with us.

One thing that Edith really loved was to come lay in the shade near the water tap. The grass there was nice and cool to rest on. When I saw her lying there I would turn the hose on a foot or so away and let it run under her. On really hot days she loved to be hosed down. She just smiled as the cold water ran over her huge body.

One morning in early July, Edith came to the porch shortly after five o'clock to have her breakfast. She seemed to be struggling with the nipple and was unable to hold it in her mouth. I couldn't figure out what the problem was until I set the bottle down and took a good look at her. In the dim, early light I could see that Edith must have had a bad experience with a fence.

Elk and fences just don't seem to get along. Edith had evidently tried to run through the middle wires of our fence. On the way through she had caught a wire in her mouth and tore one side of it about half an inch. Far back in her throat her tongue had been severely cut and she was not able to keep it in her mouth. She was unable to nurse, the hide on her front legs had also been peeled, poor Edith. She wanted her bottles so bad.

By the evening feeding we managed to get a couple of bottles of milk in her by holding the side of her mouth and keeping her tongue in line. I thought of Felipe the year before. He managed quite well and his injury was worse than Edith's. We would manage.

Edith was not the most intelligent looking creature that I ever saw. The first impression of her was: How sweet, but how dumb she looks. For the next week or so Edith looked even dumber. I almost cried every time I looked at her with her tongue hanging out about two inches to the side. The only possible caption to put on a picture of her would be, "Duh, my name Edie." Thank goodness mouth injuries heal quickly and within days Edith was back to her normal look, semi dumb.

July seventh brought us another little mule doe. A well intentioned couple had rescued the fawn when they found her abandoned in the forest. The couple brought the little doe to us on a Sunday afternoon. They were very pleased to see that she would have a terrific place to grow up and have lots of company. They realized that they had made a mistake when they picked her up; however, they learned a valuable lesson. I am sure they will never intrude again on Mother Nature.

The fawn was introduced to the residing orphans and as usual they all welcomed her. Later that afternoon we were hit by a terrible thunderstorm. All the other fawns ran to the shelters in the pen except her. She raced around mewing and crying. Fortunately the storm passed quickly and I rushed outdoors to towel dry her and to comfort her. As I was drying her off, the clouds parted and the little fawn became known as Raindoe.

Five little does with a cow elk for a big sister. Things seem to get stranger every year. I was extremely apprehensive about letting the little group out to explore the yard. After what had happened the previous year I decided to let them grow up a little. The pen was not crowded as it was last year with the bakers dozen. They would get restless and let me know when it was time.

34

THE GIRLS CLUB

On July sixteenth, the U.S. Mail delivered a special package, another little doe from Lamar, Colorado. A young boy had found the fawn with a broken leg, splinted it and taken her to the wildlife office. The truck was on a late schedule so Tom did not arrive home with her until after nine that night.

Early the next morning I took the fawn and little Midgey to visit the vet. Midgey was stronger now and ready for any consequences that she might have to face because of her severed foot. I left the two of them at the veterinary clinic and went to do some errands. I knew what they were going to tell me when I returned and tried not to think about it as I did my shopping.

In about an hour I returned to pick them up. The new little fawn was now wearing a cast and the prognosis looked good. Midgey would have to have her leg amputated in the very near future. The new little fawn was to have her cast changed in two weeks. I made an appointment to bring the two back. Midgey would have her surgery the same day. There was no other alternative.

The new little fawn didn't trust us immediately. Instead of running to us for her bottle, she would run away and hide. I was dreading the day that I would have to take the two back to town. I don't like stressing the fragile little creatures, especially her. She didn't trust us anyway.

Why is it that when you are looking forward to doing something time seems to drag on? On the other hand, why does it pass so quickly when you are dreading what has to be done? The two weeks sailed by and the morning came when I would have to take the fawns to the vet. We fed them about six o'clock and then I did my other early morning chores. I wanted to get them there early and get it over with as soon as possible.

Tom and I went into the pen to get Midgey and the new fawn that had not yet been named. It seemed that we hardly knew her. We can't give them a name until we really get to know them and their unique personalities. As I entered the shelter all six little does were neatly settled indoors relaxing and chewing their cuds. Each one seemed to have a special place of her own.

Tom laughed and said, "I see all the girls are in the DOEmitory." The little shed in the corner had been the home of many priceless creatures. When Sugar, the little antelope, used the shelter we called it the "Sugar Shack". To Larry and Elmer the elk it was known as the "Elks Lodge." To Jessica and her family it became "Fawn Hall".

I scooped up the tiny little Midge and Tom carried the other fawn to the carrier in the back of my truck. I talked to them all the way to town. We arrived shortly after eight o'clock. To my dismay the vet said that they would not be ready to go home until about twelve thirty that afternoon.

I was in no form of mind to do errands and go grocery shopping, but I did my best. I tried killing as much time as I could but finished everything by ten thirty. I decided to go by the clinic and see how things were going. As I entered the office I could hear the two fawns mewing and crying from the back room. They had not even looked at them yet. I couldn't possibly look at another item in a store so I drove the thirty miles home to wait.

They were ready to come home when I called at twelve thirty. When I went in to get them, the little one with the broken leg was waiting in the carrier and was very frightened.

I looked around. Where was Midgey? Midge was resting in one of the dog kennels, still a bit groggy from the anesthetic. As I knelt on the floor to take her in my arms tears blurred my eyes. I knew then why I had waited so long to have this done. I tried to convince myself that it was the only solution.

Her tiny back leg had been amputated at the hip. Half her body had been shaved for the procedure. Where once had been a healthy leg was now a six inch fold of skin. I do not have a weak stomach. What I saw was not that upsetting. What was bothersome was that it had to be done to my beautiful little Midgey.

Midgey

The vet explained that the severity of the amputation was to keep her from using a short leg or even a partial one. If he had left any leg at all she would use it as a crutch, never allowing it to heal. She would always have an open sore that would make her very susceptible to infection.

All three of us were anxious to get home. I was sure that they would be glad to be back in the security of their pen with their friends. I was right. When we carried the little ones into the pen, everyone came out to greet them. The two melted into the group and bedded down until evening.

Midgey was doing incredibly well very soon after her surgery. She already was able to get around the pen on three legs. It would take time for her to build up strength in the back leg that now had to do the work of two.

She would tire easily, especially while taking her bottle. With all the competition at feeding time, Midge held her own. If she tired she simply sat down to nurse. I worried about her, but decided to stick to my original plan for this summer. I was going to take one day at a time.

35

THE FOX DUMP

Rufie and Rufieanne were fascinated with the fawns. They never gave up trying to get into the pen. Every time I thought that I had the pen fox proofed, they would find the tiniest opening and excavate until they could slither their lean little bodies inside. Oh, it was fun to scare these spotted little animals! The fawns were more tolerant of the two pests than I expected them to be. If they stood their ground the pesky foxes wouldn't find much fun in the game and go somewhere else.

Nothing of value was ever to be left outdoors. The two were the biggest thieves I ever saw. Shoes were one of their favorite items. They never took both of them. It was more fun to watch us limp around with one shoe on, mumbling to ourselves while searching for the other. Of course they never just stole them, they chewed them up first.

Another treasured item as far as foxes are concerned is kitchen towels. While sitting outdoors reading one day, Tom announced that Rufie had just whizzed by with a blue towel. A few minutes later the scene was repeated, only this time the towel was yellow, scene three, brown.

I had no idea where they were taking their loot. Occasionally I would find a shoe in the llama pen, but never any of the other stolen goods. I considered changing their names to Loot and Pillage.

One evening I was coming out of the deer pen after feeding the fawns. A fox blitzed out of nowhere and in mid air snagged a baby bottle right out of my container. "You little #@&*$%#, give me that!" I needed the bottle and I ran after him. He disappeared into the thick scrub oak. I got down on my hands and knees and crawled through the net like branches determined to get my bottle back.

In a clearing in the center of the scrub oak, I discovered the "fox dump". Everything that they had ever ripped off was strewn in front of me. Ruff proudly sat there looking at me with his smiling fox eyes. There were my towels. There were two shoes, but oddly enough not a matched pair. There were the coons' flannel baby blankets. There were all of their stuffed toys. There were things that I didn't recognize.

I managed to retrieve the baby bottle and my missing towels and was able to crawl back out of the dump without too many bleeding wounds. I never went back in there again. Somehow I feel that it is a sacred place for foxes.

36

THE BEAUTIES AND THE BEAST

It was now the latter part of July. Midgey was getting along great on her three little legs. It was time for the fawns to start spending time outside their enclosure.

One morning when we went out to feed, all the fawns except our new little doe came to nurse. Over the past two weeks she had come to trust us and had started coming to us instead of making us go to her. That morning, she stayed in the shelter as the others fed. I had seen this happen so many times in the past. The last two weeks of her life had been very stressful. The broken leg, the long journey to us, another trip to the vet had worn her down to where she could not fight off infection. Usually pneumonia is the cause of their death. I knew this was happening when I saw her.

At this point all that we can do for them is to make them as comfortable as possible. Within a few hours the little doe, who we really never got to know, went to sleep on a soft thick comforter in the quiet intensive care room. Although we can't expect to save every creature that finds its way into our care and into our hearts, it is never easy to loose one.

The next morning we decided to let the girls out to explore. After breakfast, Midgey, Raindoe, Doezer, Annie and Abbie took their first step into a vast new world. Edith was on hand to meet the little friends that she had visited with through the chain link fence. She excitedly hovered around them, willing to escort them around the larger playground.

The little herd stayed close to each other while they wandered about the yard nibbling and sampling the different grasses. Edith Ann followed them around as though she was showing them the tastiest things to try. Some of the younger fawns returned to the pen and settled down for the day. The older ones disappeared into the thick oak brush to nap. Since they were spending more time out of the pen we bottle fed only twice a day: once in the morning before freeing them and then again about six in the evening to get them to return to the safety of the enclosure for the night.

It was going to be very difficult for me to start leaving them out at night. Since they were so cooperative about the routine, I decided that I would continue doing it until it was no longer possible. The events of last summer were still fresh in my mind. At least I knew where they were. They were still so young and so vulnerable. With only the six of them the pen was not as overcrowded as it had been last year with thirteen fawns.

37

IT'S A BOY!!

By the first part of August it was time to release the five little skunks and the seven raccoons that we had cared for since late spring. I happen to be one of those strange people who view skunks as perfectly harmless creatures. I really do like them and don't mind having them live in the barn. They are beneficial because they are great mousers and eat a lot of insects. We do not have dogs that bother them. The only time they are offensive is during their mating season when they do not hesitate to spray each other. We also have raccoons and foxes that try to get a bit friendly with them, but they usually learn their lesson quickly.

The five black and white beauties were getting restless in their cage in the barn. One evening while watching them try to escape I decided to open their cage to see what they would do. Usually we relocate our skunks to more remote areas so that we don't upset any of the neighbors (I hope none of them read this) but we took exception to the rule this time.

I walked over and opened the cage door then stepped back to watch. The bottom of the door was about seven inches from the ground and the little things couldn't figure out how to get out. They milled around in a little group and I could just hear what they were saying. "What do we do? How do we get out of here? We don't know? How do we do it?" They were never going to figure this out so we decided to help.

We put a wide board inside the cage for them to use as a ramp to walk up. Another board was then placed as a ramp to go down to the barn floor. Again we sat back and watched. "What do we do? How do we get out of here? We don't know!" They seemed to be mumbling to each other as they continued to mill around in a tight little group.

Finally, the oldest member of the gang figured out how to escape. He scrambled up the ramp to the doorway and then down the other ramp to freedom. The confusion inside continued so I went to their rescue. I lifted each by the tail and set them through the door. Everything went fine until the last one managed to spray me right on the mouth. I don't even know if I set him down before I wiped my mouth with the back of my hand.

They all scurried under the large wooden box in the back corner of the barn and as far as I know they still live there. Boy did I smell great! I managed to scrub the odor off with a strong soap solution. I still think it was better than getting bitten.

On August seventh we decided that it was time for the seven rotund raccoons to be on their merry way. Steve and Tom and I drove them to an isolated wildlife area that had tremendous raccoon habitat. They, as all the raccoons that we have raised, were more than ready to be on their own.

When we returned home from releasing the coons, a game warden whom we had never met before was waiting for us in the driveway. He had confiscated a deer fawn from someone who had stolen it from his mother and twin. The person wanted to have a pet deer and had been raising the fawn in their home. The little buck had even been taken on a two week car trip to California. He was brought to us and the person involved was given a very large fine.

It was obvious that the little buck had been around people all of his life. He, like big burly John from the previous year, wanted to be around people more than the other deer. Our six little does and Edith Ann were very independent. The only time that we had anything to do with them was when they needed to be fed or handled for emergency situations.

The little herd of does accepted him immediately. He soon learned that he was not going to get any more attention than any of the others. He was a strange looking little fellow. It took a while before I could come up with a name for him. It finally occurred to me. He had been to California. All the girls loved him. What else could he be called but, the Fawns. Fawnzy became his name.

38

FIDDLER GOES TO SUMMER CAMP

Fiddler had finally evolved into an almost normal raccoon. She was now spending more time away from home, however, not enough time to put the screens back on the doors. We would go for several days at a time without seeing her. Occasionally she would show up in the morning and play with Edith Ann and the foxes before retiring for the day. I didn't know where she was spending her time now that she had moved off the roof.

One evening, about supper time, our friend Eric called. Eric is the manager of a church camp about a mile from our home. He is also a very strong supporter of our efforts to raise and release our wild creatures.

He was concerned about a raccoon that had been found in a storage shed that two boys were cleaning. The raccoon had been startled by the boys and was causing a real commotion. They thought that perhaps the coon was giving birth or was injured. Would we please come see if there was anything that we could do?

Patient Tom gathered up heavy leather gloves, a noose pole and our pet carrier and drove off to see what the problem was. A short time later, Tom drove back into the yard and I went out to see what had happened. Out came the gloves, out came the noose pole, and out came the empty carrier. "What happened?" I asked. His reply was simply, "It's Fiddler."

Fiddler had found the shed to be a very comfortable dwelling. Plenty of old bedding and mattresses made a terrific home. Eric said she was welcome to stay as long as she liked if I would send a parent permission slip. After her discovery of the wonderful storage shed we only saw Fiddler a few more times.

39

DONNIE'S DAY CARE CENTER

Of all the fawns we raised the year before, I thought Henrietta would be the one to stay with us and help with the new fawns. Henrietta always stayed with Donnie when he was small. Maybe she just got tired of babysitting.

The little ones were eager to come out of the pen in the morning after their feeding. I kept a close watch on Midgey, hoping that she wouldn't venture too far. She was not going to feel sorry for herself because of her handicap. Everywhere that her friends went, she did too.

One morning she was eating grain and Rufie snuck up behind her and nipped her on the leg. In a flash, the little doe kicked the fox with her one back leg hard enough that I could hear the impact. It sounded like she broke his jaw. He didn't stay around to find out what hit him. Off he went like a streak. Midgey just kept on grazing as though nothing had happened. "Take that you stupid fox!"

The next morning, Midge was out grazing again. As she nibbled the grasses, Rufie sat behind her, at a safe distance, and seemed to be studying her rear end. "Wow! How did she do that?" Rufie never bothered the Midget again.

Throughout the month of August and into September Donnie supervised the fawns and Edith Ann. All of them loved him. For a while he would pester them, but it was only his way of proving his dominance. They accepted him as their superior.

Occasionally Artie and Gwen and Henry would drop by in the morning. John disappeared about the middle of July. The game warden that brought John would be very proud of the way that the yearling buck returned to his wild nature. John was the deer that the game warden was so concerned about because he had spent the first month of his life living in someone's home. I firmly believe that if they are given the choice that they will live where they were meant to. Although it has been several months since we have seen him, I know that I will recognize him if he comes to feed in the yard this winter.

The last day of August was the day that we had to return to our teaching jobs. It was so much easier this year than last. The summer had been very relaxing and we felt good about what we had accomplished the past three months.

I have no idea what it would be like to sleep past 5:00 A.M. Now that school had begun we had to complete all morning chores before we left home at six forty-five. That meant feeding Edith Ann on the front porch by five thirty. While feeding her I was usually met by Rufie and Rufieanne for a carry out serving of chicken. While Edith drank her bottles of milk Donnie ate his bowl of apples.

Next on the morning agenda I would go to the barn to let Milk Bone, our latest raccoon, out of his cage for the day. As I fed the llamas the little coon followed me around to help. After the llamas were taken care of, I returned to the house to get the container of warm bottles to feed the six fawns and release them from the pen for the day. Before we left for work all water containers were freshly filled, all bird feeders replenished, and the cat was put in the greenhouse for the day. In addition to the catering service, we also showered and dressed ourselves.

As we drove out of the yard I yearned to stay home at least until everyone was bedded down for the day. We were always anxious to come home in the evenings to see them all. The routine was repeated before nightfall when the coon was returned to his cage and the fawns put in the pen for the night.

40

THE BIRD LADY AND THE CHICKEN

Over the last several years of our rehabilitation efforts we have had the opportunity to raise and release many species of birds. Tom and I have always loved animals and were very excited when our vet introduced us to the "Bird Lady". The Bird Lady is a tiny, dedicated lady who has devoted more than thirty years of her life to raising orphan birds and mammals. She has raised nearly every species of bird native to our area. She has more patience than anyone I have ever known. Tiny newborn birds and mammals are her specialty.

Knowing of our fondness for wildlife, our vet suggested that we contact Glenna Beck, better known as the Bird Lady. Our very first wildlife orphan was a baby skunk that Glenna placed in our custody. After the arrival of the little skunk things just seemed to mushroom. Soon we were caring for baby robins, blue jays, grackles, magpies, crows, bunnies, squirrels and many other feathered and furred orphans. We were hooked.

Soon the animals that were brought to us were much larger. Bears, deer, antelope and even a young mountain lion added to our growing list. We decided that it was time to look for a more spacious place to live.

After our move to the foothills of the Front Range we began to care for more mammals than birds. Some of my favorite memories are of the orphan birds that we have raised. Even though we live more than thirty miles from each other, the Bird Lady and we still work closely, helping each other out whenever needed.

This past summer on the Fourth of July, a nest of red tail hawks was found by hikers. The mother and one of the chicks were dead. The surviving chick was near death and its starving little body was already covered with maggots.

Within a month, Glenna had worked her miracles and had nurtured the nestling into a young, healthy bird ready to begin leaving the nest. At this time the fledgling was brought to us. Mariah, as Glenna had named her, was totally self feeding and needed more room to exercise and learn to fly.

For the first few days she was kept in the intensive care room. I put large perches and stumps in the room for her to jump back and forth on to exercise her wings. She could simply sidestep across the perch and stare out the window.

Since the bear cage was vacant, Mariah became the new tenant. She sidestepped to the front of the cage and stared out at the vast world that she would soon experience. She loved to watch the tiny hummingbirds hover at the feeder near her cage. Mariah intently studied everything from grasshoppers to llamas.

When she wasn't standing on her perch studying, she would lie on her belly on a raised platform in the back of the cage. Even in this more comfortable position she could still memorize everything she saw. When I would approach her she would turn her head completely upside down and cluck, a soft "cluck, cluck, cluck". We nicknamed the wonderful bird "Chicken".

One morning after the foxes, deer and raccoons had retired for the day; we opened the door of her cage to see what she would do. She studied the open door but made no attempt to leave and after about an hour I closed it. A few days later we tried again. This time she hopped down on the floor of the cage and jumped through the doorway into the sunshine. The warm morning sun must have felt wonderful on her large feathered body. Chicken lay flat on her stomach and stretched her wings out to the side as far as she could reach, feeling the cool earth under her body and the warm rays of the sun on her feathered back. After a few minutes of sunbathing, she hopped back into her study for the rest of the day.

The next day she flew several feet and landed on Tom's motorcycle and studied it until the sun was too hot for her. I returned her to her cage. We tried again the next morning. This time she flew to the woodpile in the driveway and perched on the very top. Her study time was interrupted by Rufie. "What was he doing up this late?" Little troublemaker!!!

The Chicken didn't think much of the sly fox boring holes in her with his beady little eyes and flew to the top of my truck. I tried to catch her and return her to the cage until the pest retired for the day. Chicken, however, had other ideas.

The large bird lifted herself from the truck and flew off. She had never flown more than ten feet. I was shocked as I stood in the driveway and watched Chicken soar out of the yard and out of sight. "Chicken, Chicken, come back," I called. She had finally reached the point in her life when she was ready to leave the nest. The Chicken was now a fledgling.

The Chicken

I ran around the greenhouse to see where she had gone. I had no idea where she went, later that afternoon I saw her perched in a large pinion tree in the yard. From the tree I saw her fly across the road and land on the ground to feed on grasshoppers. I really thought that she would show up in the evening and return to her cage. Chicken didn't come back. Chicken had left. She had studied the situation and made her break.

I have no idea what she did during her absence, but four days later Tom returned minutes after leaving the yard on his motorcycle. I wondered why he returned so quickly and went out to see if something was wrong. "Come, quick! The Chicken is up the road perched on a rock." I jumped on the back of his bike and away we went to see her. There she was. A magnificent bird of prey, trusting us and letting us approach her as she clucked her soft little cluck and tilted her head. She had obviously been doing well on her own. After a few minutes she spread her wings and flew away.

The Chicken started making regular appearances closer to the yard. One day I saw her sitting on a large rock about two hundred yards from the house. I thought it would be a nice gesture to take her a snack. I got a frozen mouse and a frozen bird, thawed them in the microwave, and marched up the road with my offering. I held the mouse out to her beak and to my surprise; she let out a scream and snatched the food out of my hand with her foot. The only problem was that she had my finger along with the mouse. For a few moments we played tug of war and she finally let go of my finger. With her dinner in her talons she flew off to dine by herself.

From that time on when I offered her something to eat, the food was placed on a rock and I kept my distance. Again we were back to prying rabbits off the highway to feed to the Chicken. She wasn't totally dependent on us for food, but I liked to have something on hand when she did decide to pay us a visit.

It was spectacular to see her fly. We would see her sailing over the mountains that we loved. How often I wished that I could fly and see what she was seeing and feel the way she must. It was a wonderful feeling to watch her and know that the magnificent bird had been a part of our life. She was a personal friend.

One Sunday morning when she called on us, I tossed a car hit squirrel out in the yard. She soared down off the roof and carried the rodent with her foot into the safety of the scrub oak to eat. After about an hour I went out to see what was left of the squirrel. I knew she had finished eating because I could no longer see her. I never bothered her when she ate. As I squatted on the ground examining the remains of her dinner I heard a soft "cluck, cluck, cluck." A few feet away from me was the Chicken, nestled in the shade of the scrub, completely camouflaged, digesting her dinner.

The Chicken was part of the regular routine again. Only now she was free and could choose when and if she wanted to visit us. As we drove up the road returning from school each day, we would both scan the area to see who could catch sight of her first. One of her favorite places to wait for us was on the railing on the deck off our bedroom. Her visits became less frequent and we were pleased that she was finally getting better at hunting her own food.

She had been gone for five days. Perhaps she had migrated down the mountain and onto the plains. The food that I had for her was put back in the freezer to thaw out for the next creature that would need it.

We missed her. When we drove into the yard in the evening we both felt emptiness when we no longer saw her waiting in her favorite places.

On a warm late summer hike with the llamas we watched a large hawk gliding along the tops of the enormous pine trees. We both silently wondered to ourselves if it could possibly be our predator friend.

After our morning walk I went inside to bake some cookies. The peaceful morning was broken by a scream. A few seconds later another scream. "What in the world is that?" I asked Tom. I went out the front door and he went out the back. "The Chicken is back!" I heard him say. I ran around the house to see her. Sure enough, she was perched on top of the house demanding her Sunday dinner.

A few days later when we drove into the yard, I noticed the llamas staring at something. I went to see what was so interesting. The Chicken was on the ground and would suddenly lift herself up about four feet and then land again. She kept repeating this action. She was lifting and dropping a large bullsnake. I suppose she was trying to kill it, but was not dropping the snake far enough to hurt it. As I got close to her she flew up onto a fence post and I grabbed the snake and stuck it under the woodpile. I then went in the house and got her a road killed rabbit. At least she knew what she was supposed to be doing.

Fall was rapidly approaching and we wondered whether the beautiful red tail hawk would migrate for the winter. Only time would tell us.

41

MILKBONE

On the twenty-first of August Tom made a two hundred mile drive to pick up another orphan raccoon. The young coon was being sent to us by the veterinary clinic in Cheyenne, Wyoming that two years earlier had sent us Gracie, the clumsy red fox.

The little coon had been at the clinic since it was only a few weeks old. The time had come to find him a home where he could learn to be wild. We felt complimented that they would send him such a great distance so that he could do his raccoon internship with us.

He fit right in with the rest of the orphans. Everyone seemed to know that he had a right to live with us and accepted him as part of the scene. It didn't take long to give him a fitting name. He was crazy about Milkbone dog biscuits, sorting them out of his food dish before tasting anything else. He loved all the flavors. Milkbone was a very appropriate name for the new raccoon.

Milkbone was allowed the freedom of the yard during the day. At night he was returned to the safety of his cage. I remembered what had happened to Vidal the year before. Milkbone would be a larger coon before he was left out to fend for himself during the night. One bobtail coon is enough.

Vidal was still dropping in for handouts after dark. If I wasn't outside when she arrived, she would come to the back door, open it and then slam it. I always had something to give her. She had to be the nicest raccoon that we have ever been around.

Her attitude changed the night that she came home and discovered that Milkbone was living in her territory. I hadn't put Milkbone up for the night when Vidal arrived and met the little coon in the barn. "Ooiee, ooiee, ooiee," must be raccoon language for "You better get out of my sight." I managed to grab Milkbone and lift him off the ground while Vidal lunged at him. I shoved him in his cage and slammed the door. "Whew!" Vidal was not going to forgive me. I was actually afraid of her.

She was trying to eat me alive and had already started on my feet. I grabbed the closest thing that I could get my hands on, which happened to be a broom. I used the broom to keep her away from me as I inched myself toward the house. I made it to the door and squeezed inside, shaking her off my pant leg before I slammed the door in her face.

With her visiting regularly I now had to be exceptionally careful about putting Milkbone up before she arrived. I guess she finally forgave me. The next time she came she was the nice coon that I had always known. Vidal had grown into a beautiful adult. She was paying us regular visits so that she could fatten up for the coming winter.

We had known her for more than a year. It was a real compliment to us that she would still trust us, yet be wild enough to take off for long periods of time. I'm sure she will have a family of her own this spring. Perhaps Milkbone will play an important part in her life someday. For the time being the rowdy little coon was still caged at night.

42

ON PINS AND NEEDLES

August twenty-ninth was our last day of freedom. Tomorrow we would have to return to school. Early in the day Lee called to tell me that a woman would be bringing in an orphan porcupine. We had never had a baby porcupine and I prayed all day long that the little one would be self feeding so that I could take care of it. If it needed to be fed at frequent intervals the little orphan would have to go to the Bird Lady until milk feedings were needed only twice a day.

The little cactus arrived at the wildlife office right at closing time. Lee called me immediately and said that the small mammal had not eaten anything for at least twenty four hours. I knew that the best thing would be to send the porcupine to Glenna. She had the time to get the little animal off to a good start. I could hardly wait for the day to arrive when the baby would be transferred to us.

Two weeks later the spiny little creature came to live with us. She was now starting to eat leaves and bark all by herself and milk feedings were only necessary twice a day. Another chore was added to the morning agenda. I now had to feed the little porcupine with an eyedropper. It reminded me of Sweet Potato, the beaver that we raised last summer. The two had many similar characteristics. They even complained the same.

Quilma

When I arrived at her cage at five thirty in the morning I would call her and she would come out of her house eager to have her milk. As I sat on the floor of her cage she would hold my finger with one of her exquisite little feet and sit up taking eyedropper after eyedropper of milk until it was all gone. When she finished eating she wanted to climb on me and cuddle. How do you cuddle a porcupine? Her round little tummy and soft face were the only parts of her body that didn't have quills. I would slip my hand under her and nuzzle her face with mine. She loved it and didn't want to be put down. I would have liked to cuddle more also, but I had other things to do before we left for work.

When I set her down in the cage she would throw a temper tantrum. I never saw anything quite like it. She would sit up on her hind legs and hold her front legs up in front of her face, then mechanically toss her head back and forth in the opposite direction that her two front feet were going. "Don't go! Don't go!" she seemed to be telling me.

In the evening I again fed her with the eyedropper and then spent more time with her, letting her climb on me and touch my face and hair. Baby porcupines must get a lot of attention from their mothers because only one baby is born to the mother after a gestation period of seven months. This is an incredibly long time for such a small mammal.

As the weeks passed she began eating bark from several varieties of trees and bushes. She was also very fond of apples and still very dependent and clingy after her milk feedings. We named the little pin cushion "Quilma". It was going to be very exciting watching her grow up.

43

SUMMER BEARLY COMES TO AN END

I had good intentions to wean my babies by the middle of September, well, maybe once a day feedings by the end of September or maybe October. "Oh, what the heck," how can you take something away from them that they enjoy so much? As long as they wanted to drain the bottles I would keep on filling them.

Edith decided that one bottle a day was sufficient, and she chose to have it in the evening. As I stepped out the door with her bottle, she and the six fawns would converge on the porch. It didn't take long for the little ones to realize that they couldn't compete with the giant towering above them. They would retreat to the grain bowl while Edie guzzled her twenty-eight ounce bottle.

Cecilia & Edith

After Edith finished I would go indoors and get the bottles for the little ones. When we returned outside we would trip and stumble over them as they danced around our feet. We would put them in the pen to feed them and close the gate for the night.

Edith had a voracious appetite. If she wasn't eating grain, she was eating apples. If she wasn't eating oak leaves, she was in the barn picking out the tenderest leaves from the choice bales of alfalfa hay. If she wasn't vacuuming the bird feeding saucers, she was chewing on the license plates on Tom's truck. I called her Edie the Gourmet.

Edie had her own circle of friends. When the mule deer that weren't in her social class tried to sneak into the yard for a snack, Edie would pin her ears back and chase them away. They would take one look at the huge creature coming at them and bound out of her yard. One evening I even saw her chasing the large bucks out of the llama pasture. By October, Edith Ann weighed well over two hundred pounds. She made her lifelong friend, Donnie, look small when they stood side by side.

Donnie had matured into a spectacular yearling. It was hard to believe that he was the scrawny little fawn that we pampered only one year ago. Donnie was fat and he deserved every ounce of fat that he had stored on his body. He wouldn't shiver this coming winter that was for sure.

Henrietta would disappear for weeks at a time and then saunter into the yard when least expected and stay for a few days. Hopefully, Henry would get pregnant this fall and decide to be a real deer. The rest of last years fawns had finally made the transition into the wild deer herd. I really believe that they never forget us and what we had done for them. Each had a special mark or characteristic that enables us to recognize them as the unique individuals that they are.

I guess Donnie was going to live with us for awhile yet. Perhaps when the rut began, he would have more important things on his mind. Why should he leave now? He was already in charge of his own little herd of does.

Deer Ann, Deer Abby, Raindoe, Doezer, Midgey and the Fawns were now out of spots. We have learned a lot over the past several years. Our approach this year seemed to pay off. Our little group of fawns was the most independent that we have ever had. They had not been around anyone except Tom and me. I really tried not to attach myself as personally as I had in the past. Still, each was special and each was respected for the unique personality that they had been endowed with.

Deer Abby, our only whitetail of the season, again exhibited the differences between the two species. She was more wary, more sophisticated and more egotistical than the mule deer. Abby brought back so many beautiful memories of my magical Jessica. Perhaps she too, will share her offspring with us.

Deer Ann was the explorer of the group. She was the fortunate little doe that was found by the family of tourists. They had taken time out of their vacation to find help for the little fawn with a broken leg. I wished that I had gotten their name so I could let them know that she was doing so well. I can still see her as a tiny fawn, hobbling along in her stiff little cast, always wondering what it was like OUT THERE. She was finding out what it was like, and thanks to the thoughtful vet, she is able to do it on four healthy legs.

Doezer, my tomboy, was the first to don the healthiest winter coat that I have ever seen on a fawn. She never went through the shaggy late summer look. Over night, she seemed to mature into a beautiful young lady. Doezer supported my theory about the deer that come from Lamar. Every one of them has been big boned and hardy.

Raindoe, since the day that she came to us has kept the sun shining and rainbows in the sky. The shy, carefree little doe was the last to loose her camouflage coat. Raindoe was Midgey's closest friend. Every time I see a rainbow I will think of the mewing, frightened little doe in the thunderstorm.

Fawnzy was now sprouting half inch antlers. The little buck adjusted well to the world in which he was born. His travels would now take him to green, grassy meadows and sheltered mountain slopes instead of car trips to California.

Midgey was the most cherished fawn of the year. Her little shaved hip had grown a winter coat before her spots had vanished. By the end of September the awkward patch blended in with her fine, warm winter coat. Again we had a wonderful vet to thank for helping. The surgery that he had performed on the little doe was cost free to us. Since we are not funded in anyway for our care of wildlife this meant a great deal to us.

Maybe it was because of her handicap that Midge knew that she had to be exceptionally cautious. When the little herd left for the day, Edith and the five little ones would trickle back to the yard alone or in pairs. Midgey would wait until dusk to come home. I will never forget the first night that everyone was present for dinner except little three legged Midgey. With a heavy heart I fed the others and wondered where she was. Had the coyotes gotten her as I feared they would? As I was leaving the pen and closing the gate, I saw the llamas, who I call my "Silent Gossips", staring intently at something in their pasture.

My heart lifted as I watched tiny Midgey stotting (stiff legged bounding) toward the pen. With a sigh of relief I gave her a bottle and let her in with her friends for the night.

Midgey was the first to find shelter when enormous Edith had the urge to chase and play with anyone who was brave enough. The scene reminded me of a pool table. The little fawns would be grazing in the front yard, then suddenly Edith would blast through the middle, scattering the fawns like billiard balls, ricocheting and darting to the safety of the pockets of the scrub oak. If I happened to be in the vicinity during the game, Midgey would run for safety and stand motionless between my legs.

Unlike Larry, Edith never invited me or Tom to play her games. I never feared for my health or my life with Edith as I did with Larry. Despite her size, she had very good manners. Except for her sporadic episodes, Edith was a gentle giant. The beautiful creature seemed as though she had always been with us. I wondered how she would choose to leave us.

Rufie and Rufieanne were not living in the yard anymore. I didn't know where they were staying but imagined that the way the two kept house it would not be too difficult to find their new home. I really didn't want to know. They were beginning their normal lives. In the summer the two would come to the yard each evening and raise havoc with whatever they could. I loved to watch them chase and play. They would stand up and box with each other and roll and wrestle in the tall grass. It must be wonderful to be a fox.

By late summer I began to notice that Rufieanne was physically changing. She obviously was not a female. Rufie was still touchable at times so I grabbed her one evening and sure enough, Rufie was a girl. The two were making separate trips to the yard. I'm sure that it was some perverted little fox trick to try to confuse me. From a distance I couldn't tell which one it was and just about the time I thought I knew, both of them would appear.

Little Rufie, who played in the house just a few months ago was now a young adult. She would probably have a family of her own in the spring. Her brother, who was always untouchable, was now as sly a fox as you could imagine. What a wonderful experience to watch them evolve into wild creatures. Would we be able to observe them through the winter as we had Gracie?

The Chicken was getting more independent. She now only came to the yard about once a week. She usually made a Sunday afternoon appearance. Now when I tossed a piece of meat to her, she would scan the area thoroughly before accepting it. Once she had it in her talons she would fly off to eat in privacy.

One Sunday, about noon, I had just driven into the yard and gotten out of the car. Tom came out of the house to meet me and we both heard a scream. The beautiful hawk soared over us and hovered as she called to us. The sound that she made sent chills down my spine.

Two weeks later we were visited by the first frost of the year. We have not seen her since. Perhaps the change of weather sent her on her winter journey. Would she return in the spring?

Fall was only a few days away. In a conversation with my neighbor one day, she stated that it would be nice if we didn't have to winter any large animals this year. I agreed that it certainly would make things easier.

On September twenty-first, Tom received a call at school. A bear cub had been seen regularly on a golf course in a town about a hundred miles away. The cub had been orphaned six weeks earlier when a home owner had shot and killed its mother. The residents living around the golf course became concerned for the safety of the cub. Before she could get herself into trouble, wildlife officials trapped her and asked us to keep her for the winter.

The cub was relayed to us the same day and we picked her up at the wildlife office on our way home from work. She was tranquilized while in the bear trap and then the sleepy little orphan was placed in our carrier for her journey to her winter home.

When we got home we were able to determine her sex and weigh her while she peacefully slept. The little bear weighed only twenty-nine pounds. She would have had a tough time making it through the winter months on her own.

A sibling was also seen, but the two had separated. I had a feeling that when cold weather set in, we would be wintering the two of them. The high society golf course cub became known as Rona Bearet. Within three weeks Rona was turning into a roly poly black bear.

Mid October found us facing the hunting season again. I tried to keep myself busy, which isn't too difficult around here, to keep my mind off the time of year.

Milkbone and the fawns were no longer confined at night. In the morning, as I did my chores, the chubby little coon followed me around and helped as many others had done over the years. One morning as I headed into the house to get ready for work, Milkbone met me in the driveway in the dim light. I heard a jingling sound as he tagged along. I was sorry the minute that I picked him up. The little devil was covered with the putrefying smell of fresh skunk spray. The jingling sound that I heard was a four inch fishing lure attached securely through the corner of Milkbone's mouth. "How lucky could I be?" There I was, holding a skunk drenched raccoon while he happily played with the fishing lure dangling from his mouth and it was only thirty minutes until we had to leave for work.

I headed for the house to get Tom's professional help. The two of us could not hold him still enough to snip the end off the fishhook. The only choice we had was to take him to the vet to get the job done, so I took the morning off and Tom drove us to town. At the vet's office he was given a mild tranquilizer and the fishhook was removed. The smelly coon and I were not very popular at the clinic and left when the minor operation was completed. Milkbone was wide awake and very happy to get at home. I deodorized myself and returned to work.

Rufie no longer let me get very close to her. The little red fox was getting wilder by the day. One evening she came to the yard and I noticed that her ear was bloody and hanging to one side. I tried to entice her to come closer so that I could inspect the ear, but she would have nothing to do with me. As time passed I noticed from a distance that the ear had healed well, but was obviously injured enough that it would never be straight again. It would always be crooked.

The fawns and Edith were weaned the first week of November. I had no other choice. Edith shredded all the nipples with her huge bottom teeth.

FINAL CHAPTER
WHAT YOU DO NOT KNOW
YOU FEAR

Each day of the hunting season was savagely marked off my calendar with a black marker pen. We were facing one more weekend and it would be over for another year. The last two days are the ones that we dread the most. A phone call on Friday night shattered our hopes of surviving another season without incident.

I didn't want to hear what my neighbor was telling me. "No! It's not true! Please tell me that it didn't happen, Please!" That morning he and his two year old daughter were at the irrigation pond about three quarters of a mile from our house. Donnie, Henrietta, Edith and the little fawns were in the pasture nearby. Henrietta approached the two humans. Donnie, who had matured remarkably the last two months, was now in the rut (breeding season) and saw the humans as a threat to one of his does. He challenged the man to a fight. It must have been a terrifying experience for the man and his little girl. I could tell by the sound of his voice that he was very upset and urged us to do something about the buck with the saber spikes. He wasn't angry with us, but only wanted to warn us of the potential danger.

I had heard of this happening in other hand raised bucks. They loose their fear of humans and during the rutting season will consider humans to be part of their herd. Our only choice was to put Donnie in the pen until we decided what could be done. It hurt so bad to shut him in. He had never been confined during the fourteen months that we had him. He was confused. This was a very important time in his life. Perhaps his strange behavior had something to do with the high fever that he had in the spring when he almost died.

I had worried about the little buck for the last few months. He didn't want to leave. I thought it was because of the little does that were still dependent on us. Perhaps it was, but still, I was concerned. Last year when the fawns were making

163

their very important social move into the wild herds, Donnie was only two months old and didn't move with them. I thought that in time he would also make the move as so many before him had done. I tried to avoid any kind of contact with him.

The next three weeks were horrible. Steve made several phone calls to see if Donnie could be placed on a deer breeding ranch. No one wanted him when they heard that he had been aggressive to humans. We were told that aggressive behavior toward humans would get worse as the deer matured. The only other choice that we had was to destroy him. The thought sickened us. We were totally helpless.

I tried penning him up during the day and then freeing him at night. Maybe, just maybe, he would go off with the bucks. In the morning I would put him back in the pen. A few times he wasn't home in the morning and I had no choice but to leave him out. I spent those days at work being a nervous wreck, wondering if he had bothered other humans. I couldn't live this way. It was killing me. We had to make this nightmare stop.

We had one more thing to try. His antlers were his most dangerous weapon. They loose them every year anyway. Why not saw them off? Maybe it would make him less aggressive. We obtained a cattle prod to attempt to make him afraid of humans. We would do anything to let him live.

Steve gave us a tranquilizer to perform the antler removal. Tom didn't have to use it. Donnie had always been extremely fond of Tom and nuzzled him gently as he sawed through the finger sized spikes.

We were so positive that this would work. We felt slightly relieved. Tom removed Donnie's antlers Monday night. We had two days of school before our four day Thanksgiving vacation. We could be at home and monitor the situation closely. I couldn't live with the thought of him seriously injuring or even killing someone. In casual conversation on our way to work one morning, Tom recalled part of a dream that he had the night before. All that he could remember of the dream was that a crooked ear fox had appeared and provided assurance that everything was going to be all right.

Tuesday evening I let Donnie out of the pen. To my dismay, he followed me and pestered me as though I was one of his does. The cattle prod worked like a charm. He hated it and finally left me alone. That night he left and did not return in the morning. "Please let him be gone, I prayed." I never wanted to see him again. I relaxed even more when we arrived home and he was still nowhere to be seen. Lightheartedly I prepared my Thanksgiving dinner for the next day.

Thanksgiving morning arrived and I thought of the many things that we had to give thanks for. I felt even better when I didn't see the mature yearling with the rest of the deer in the yard. Through the telescope we could see him on the hillside about half a mile away with several of the wild does. It was going to work!

My heart sunk again when I looked out about nine o'clock in the morning and saw him coming through the pasture toward home. I felt like a traitor as I left the house with the cattle prod to drive him away. "What was wrong?" he seemed to be thinking as he backed away from the shocking stick. "I have always been welcome here before." I choked back the tears as I drove him away. I was only doing it because I loved him. I should have done it months ago.

Our Thanksgiving dinner was eaten with token conversation. Our mothers and we were feeling the tension that had been nonstop for almost three weeks. The two of them left about three in the afternoon, leaving us with the worst decision that we have had to face.

Shortly after they left, Tom glanced out the window and saw a deer chasing the neighbor kids who had been out playing football after their dinner. It was Donnie. He had been attracted to a scene that would make a normal deer flee. The kids ran for the safety of the house as I ran toward them. Donnie then ran toward me and didn't seem the least bit frightened of the prod that I had used to chase him with that same morning. When he saw Tom, he relaxed and followed him into the pen. He could not be trusted. We had to do something.

Darkness set in and we sat at the kitchen table holding hands and not wanting to discuss what was going to have to be done. As I sat staring out at the darkness, a familiar shape came into view. Outside, staring directly at me was the crooked ear fox. It had been over a week since I'd seen the fox. Usually I would only see her in the mornings, never at night. I told Tom to look out and as he did tears streamed down his face. In a choking voice he said, "That was my dream."

Sleep did not come easily. We both wished that morning would never come. The snow storm that had been predicted for Thanksgiving Day had arrived during the night. When I awoke, Tom was not at my side. I knew that he had a promise to keep and could not bring myself to look outside. In a daze I dressed and went out to do my chores. As I left the back door I glanced toward the pen and saw my Tom, lying in the deep snow with the beautiful buck resting peacefully against his body. Death came silently to Donnie. He never knew that Tom gave him the tranquilizer shot that had not been used when his antlers were taken off. After a short pawing of the ground he simply lay down to rest, never to stand again. While Donnie was in deep sleep, Tom placed a glass with chloroform around his muzzle until his breathing subsided.

Edith, Henrietta and the little does stood guard outside the pen while life slipped away from their lifelong friend. In the deafening silence I caught a glimpse of Big Tim leaving our yard.

It is so strange how you can cope with what has to be done. We managed to slide his body onto our toboggan and placed two red roses from our Thanksgiving bouquet on his neck. The two of us, in silence, pulled our friend through the untouched snow to his final resting place. The blanket of white seemed to cover all traces of what we had been forced to do.

What one fears one destroys.

THE END

EPILOGUE

There are many questions raised over the ethical values of wildlife rehabilitation. Many skeptics believe that it is impossible to raise a wild animal and reintroduce it into its natural habitat. Deer are probably the most difficult animals that we work with. They imprint very easily on humans and readily learn to trust them.

Neither Tom nor I had a personal fear of Donnie. The fear that we had was of what he had done and what he was capable of doing as he matured. We had been extremely successful in rehabilitating deer for the last seven years. Perhaps our confidence was too great and we needed to be reminded of the reality of what we are trying to do.

No one likes failure. The grief that we experienced over the episode with Donnie left us having second thoughts over continuing our rehabilitation program. I guess that you can learn from not accomplishing what you set out to do. We are entrusted with these delicate little creatures and we do everything possible for their survival. Maybe we do more than we should. Is there too much interference with Mother Nature?

Donnie was a victim of circumstances. Natural selection probably would have taken him because of his late summer birth. Man interfered and he was brought to us. We believe in what we do and gave the little buck a second chance. Perhaps we interfered once too often when Donnie almost died the first spring of his life. Nature was communicating with us and we did not heed the message.

Whatever the lesson was that Donnie was sent to teach us, I know that we will continue to nurture any creature that comes our way. Before our lives are over more orphans will enchant our lives, and more little hoof prints will follow the trails to and from the security of our yard. We will share the transition into their real world and grieve when it is not meant to be. Much heartache will accompany our efforts. In the end all of us in some unexplainable way will come together again, and the togetherness will be a joyous reunion.

0-595-33065-7

Printed in the United States
22578LVS00005BB/16-18